There is a lot to be said for achieving a deep educational background and professional training to develop an intellectual understanding of neurodiversity. In *That Zen Farm*, Marcy Waelti combines her extensive knowledge with decades of experience working with both equines and humans. This book is a wonderful journey — touching, insightful, and a must for your reading list.

~ Melisa Pearce, MSW – Founder and CEO,
Touched by a Horse, Inc.

In this remarkable work, Marcy Waelti not only shares her transformational healing journey with horses, but she also recounts her path to becoming a soul whisperer as well as a horse whisperer. Her love for horses and serving others permeates the book, encouraging readers to begin — or continue — parallel journeys of their own. Her evocative writing invites readers to embrace their own neurodiversity and path to wholeness. Make no mistake: Marcy may be soft-spoken, but she is a powerhouse of compassion while graced with superb competence in horsemanship and the skill to hold space with her clients while they experience emotions, distress, or breakthroughs in their journeys. Profound questions for the "self" emerge as we read this book. The author's expression of her experience, newfound spiritual awareness, and compassion for all living things challenge us to ask deeper questions of ourselves. *That Zen Farm* is a must-read for anyone seeking guidance on their own path to wholeness, whether understanding how horses help us heal or working with neurodivergent adults or youth. This book is also essential for those seeking to become better horsemen or horsewomen. Marcy sprinkles her awareness of how horses live as sentient beings as she reflects on how they can be both our mounts and best friends.

~ Hertha Lund – Master Equine Gestalt Coach, Speaker,
Author, Horseshoer, Poet, Attorney

Marcy writes from the heart of an experienced horsewoman and from the soul of an innate healer and caregiver. She is as personal and open as she is professional and wise — all of which brings her stories vividly to life on the page. This book carries us through her journey of assisting people of all ages and abilities alongside her beloved horses, offering an intimate look inside her sweet That Zen Farm, where horses heal humans and the ripple of that work extends far beyond the arena, giving the reader a welcome splash of her healing energy. We live in an increasingly diverse world, and what a gift it is to have Marcy's insights on how we can make a greater difference in the lives of those around us.

~ Nelle Rogers – Master Equine Gestalt Coach,
Owner and Founder, Seahorse Healing LLC

Marcy is a truly gifted spirit with the rare ability to see beyond what is spoken in those she works with. She is a skilled horsewoman who is able to harness the power of the horse's intuition to create a safe, reflective place for the people she supports. Marcy's book builds an understanding of what brought her to this place through vulnerable and relatable stories of her upbringing, her career in childcare, and her extensive training that now so beautifully informs her work with neurodivergent children.

Having seen firsthand the magic that unfolds between horse and child under Marcy's guidance, it can be challenging to describe all that is happening in every micro-interaction — the dropping in, the layering of skills that are often difficult to define, the settling into self.

Marcy's book takes these concepts, which are often difficult to articulate, and lays them out in a way that reminds us of our humanness and the power of connection to create change, and with it, offers reason for hope.

The book is a gift for anyone touched by neurodiversity and who may be interested in the power of an equine-assisted approach.

~ Jennifer Bluske, OTR/L – Parent Coach, Owner,
Children's Therapy Network (Madison, WI)

ISBN: 978-1-954102-36-1 (paperback)
ISBN: 978-1-954102-37-8 (ebook)

Library of Congress Control Number: 2026942100

Printed in the United States of America

First Printing: 2026
Edited by Cameron Cowan, Beth Rule
Interior design by Amit Dey
Cover design by Veronica Coello
Cover photo credit to Heather McManamy, ShortHorse Studios

SOMETHING OR OTHER PUBLISHING
Brooklyn, Wisconsin 53521
Info@SOOPLLC.com

For bulk orders email: Orders@SOOPLLC.com

TRADEMARK ACKNOWLEDGMENT

THAT ZEN FARM

Where Horses Heal Humans

MARCY WAELTI

This work would not be possible without the wonderful help of friends and family. I dedicate this book to:

Melisa Pearce, Martha Kniffin, Denise Mirkin, Jen Bluske, Brenda Westwood, Risa August, and Hertha Lund who assisted me on my journey,

My children who taught me patience and acceptance,

And most of all my wonderful husband Dale Waelti.

CONTENTS

INTRODUCTION

"You can treat people like they are different,
or you can make a difference — the choice is yours."

~ Marcy Waelti

I'm grateful to have been able to do what I'm passionate about for most of my life. I've been told I'm more horse than human. It might be true, and it has helped me understand energy, body language, fear responses, and building trust.

There are many ways to work with all ages and stages of horses and humans. My way evolved through years of winding and seldom-intersecting paths until I enrolled in the Touched by a Horse Equine Gestalt Coaching Method (EGCM) course developed by Melisa Pearce. Only then, after fifty-five years of teaching horsemanship and training horses, did everything I had learned about horses and working with people fall into place.

Embracing the Gestalt belief that people are whole, capable, and inherently resourceful has turned what I once did naturally into a conscious practice of teaching and healing, both in my own life and in my work with clients.

In horse training and riding, I have evolved from the old "kick 'em to go and pull 'em to stop" kind of horse gal, to an oh-so-subtle use of energy and body language to accomplish the same results.

Combining these approaches into my work with children with special needs has made the journey more meaningful for all three of us.

Most of my clients these days are children on the autism spectrum. Each one is an individual learning to their best self and discovering who they are becoming. All are treated with respect and love and are given the gift of being heard. I make no assumptions about what a person can or cannot do; instead, I remain curious about what might be possible.

I also work with adults, many of whom were late-diagnosed with autism spectrum disorder (ASD) or other mental health challenges, or who received very little support in their younger years. One of the skills I've developed is the ability to really listen and ask questions that help them to better understand themselves.

The following pages are about what I do and how I do it. Will my ideas change the world of horse-and-human interactions? Will they change the world of equine therapy? I don't know. I only know that they have changed the lives of my clients, my horses, and me.

I'm listening
I hear you
With all my heart
I hear you
When we sit together
I hear you
Your words
Your soul
Your unsaid and mislaid words
Your heart
With my soul and my heart
I hear you

~ Marcy Waelti

CHAPTER ONE

THE WINDING PATH TO THAT ZEN FARM

"Creativity is a lot like looking at the world through a kaleidoscope. You look at a set of elements, the same ones everyone sees, but then reassemble those floating bits and pieces into an enticing new possibility."

~ Rosabeth Moss Kanter

That Zen Farm is located in the gently rolling hills of southern Wisconsin, USA. The Swiss-style home (with windows all around) sits on top of a hill in the middle of the horse pastures. The first thing I see each morning are horses, horses, and horses. My heart is filled with love. This place of peace was built with our hearts, souls, hands, and a lot of cash. We had a vision of a farm where people, especially children, could come and discover the love of horses.

The farm has become a place of learning, healing, and peace for all who come here. Those gentle horses can carry a person upon their backs, and they can heal without ever being ridden. Our program, Energy Connected Therapeutic Horsemanship, has developed from my years of lifelong learning and become a model for teaching and healing. It took years of twisting and winding to find the true path of my life's mission.

MY EARLY JOURNEY

I have always loved horses — always! As a child, the dolls I had were only used to ride and care for a variety of plastic and ceramic horses. I doubt that my dolls ever wore fancy clothes — they lived in jeans! There are those of us who are born with horses in our blood. I was fortunate to have parents who understood and did what they could to allow me to get my fill.

Mom was only fifteen when I was born. My dad was attending technical school in another state, and I lived with both sets of grandparents and my great-grandmother while Mom finished high school. When I was five, Mom and I moved to Houghton, Michigan, to be with Dad, where we lived in an itty-bitty trailer. I ran free, attended kindergarten, raised pollywogs to frogs, and played in the deep snow.

After Dad graduated, we moved to a bigger trailer in southern Michigan and lived there until I was about eleven years old. I had one friend — a girl with ponies. I love ponies to this day and have several in my herd. The time I spent at her farm was a piece of how I survived the things that happened to me.

One of the most influential times of my life occurred during our time in Port Huron, Michigan. Around the age of six or seven, I became "friends" with an elderly man in our trailer park. My mom would send me over with meals for him, and he would talk to me while he ate. He was a twisted old pedophile. He soon had me in his trap. He taught me things a child should never know. He had me so well trained with statues of horses as rewards that I never told anyone what he did to me until I was forty years old. During my Equine Gestalt training, I did my work around this time of my life and was shaken, awakened, and learned that I had turned that terrible time around and become a guardian of children.

We moved to Madison, Wisconsin, and spent a couple of years in a trailer park where I led a typical life as a young girl and even began to take riding lessons. When I was in sixth grade, we moved into a rental house in the country, and I was set free from the constraints of city life. I ran up and down the hill next to our house like a feral horse. I crossed the swamp by jumping from grassy hump to grassy hump, then stood in the cold creek and watched the trout and bullheads. I took care of our pets, injured wild critters, abandoned baby animals, and my siblings. Is it any wonder that my number one value is compassion for the world around me?

My mom also loved horses, and we would ride rented horses together. I remember riding in front of her in the saddle when I was very young. As I grew, I made friends with girls who had horses, and I loved riding with them. I began hunt-seat riding lessons when I was about nine years old, taught by a woman from England. She was an amazing teacher.

As my mom and I expanded our knowledge, I had several different teachers — most were good at what they did. I was so dedicated to learning that even when I didn't have transportation after school, I would walk the two miles to the stable to be with the horses. My favorite was a Hackney pony named Olé, even though he dragged me up the driveway when the electric fence went up between his back legs. It wasn't his fault. The so-called teachers who weren't good taught me how *not* to teach horses and humans. I absorbed the lessons they had for me and set aside those ideas that didn't align with my own standards.

My parents purchased a 234-acre farm around 1967. I fell in love with being a farm girl when our first Shetland ponies arrived. The next year I received my own horse, and I've never been the same since. That horse, Karada's Cherokee, took better care of me than anyone else had in my life.

By the end of that first summer, I was training other people's horses, and by fourteen I was teaching people to ride. I was active in 4-H and eventually became a youth leader. Later, when my own children were young, I served as a horse project leader in our local 4-H club. It's a wonderful program that teaches so much more than animal care. The 4-H pledge itself is a powerful example of a way to live:

I pledge…
my HEAD to clearer thinking,
my HEART to greater loyalty,
my HANDS to larger service, and
my HEALTH to better living,
for my club, my community,
my country and my world.

My children grew up in the 4-H program as well. They enjoyed cooking, baking, art, rocketry, carpentry, dog training, and showing calves and horses.

A big shift in my trust in human beings came when I was thirteen. I was babysitting my siblings when a young man (he was nineteen) whom my parents called "a family friend" came to visit. He had a very violent father, and I believe my parents thought they were showing him a better way of life.

What I found out that night was that he was another pedophile looking for young girls. He trapped me and raped me. I fought back like a tiger, and he finally left. To this day I have no real memory of what fully happened. When I was a young teen, the girl was believed to be at fault if she were raped. I told no one until I was sixteen, when my inner emotional kettle was about to boil over. My father asked what I did to bring on the attack. My mom didn't believe me and continued to allow him to come to our home, even when he tried to do the same to my sister six years later. Thankfully, my brother heard the ruckus and chased him away with a knife.

The trauma of my violation made it very difficult to have normal fun with boys. I found boys and men, especially in a dating scenario, very frightening. There was one boy from our neighborhood who didn't scare me. Dan loved his horse and riding, and we would join the neighborhood kids on their horses for day-long trail rides. I felt safe because my valiant steed kept me off the ground where I was vulnerable. I did try to have a boyfriend in high school, but it didn't last long. My fears made that impossible.

My parents were having a rough time with each other by the time I was fifteen, and the stress of living in their chaotic energy was too much for me. I moved myself, my loyal miniature dachshund, and my best horse friend, Karada's Cherokee, to a valley in the depths of our farm to get as far away from things as I could. We camped in the hollow at the base of four hills in an old tent. We had half an acre of grass surrounded by trees, birds, squirrels, gophers, rabbits, a fire pit, and a freshwater spring. The grass was sweet, and so was life as I settled in each night.

During the day, I would go back to the farm to train horses, teach lessons, get food, and take a shower. I stayed away from the rest of my family unless I had to take care of my siblings. Dad left us when I was about sixteen. He left with no goodbyes. It was a painful and confusing summer. Mom was acting like a teenager left off the leash. That is when I added taking care of my mom to the list of those I cared for.

I was nineteen when I became engaged. He was the first person I spoke to about what happened to me after the heartbreaking failure of my parents to believe me. I put my trust in him. He was very patient and loving with me until I was comfortable. I still had trouble being in a room with other men, but I shoved it down and coped. I survived these crashes in my trust of a "friend" and my parents because I have a great deal of resilience. Knock me down and I will get up again, and again. I have a great group of Gestaltists who assisted me to wholeness and are my steadfast friends.

Many years later, during my work to become fully whole and healed at the EGCM program, I expunged the rapist from my body and soul. I now work with many young men who have had violent pasts and are struggling to find their own true paths. I often wonder if the men who hurt me would have turned out differently if they had received help.

I never rested on my journey to learn more. I took on more challenges, new teachers, and read books and magazines on every facet of horses. I was never long without the one stable aspect of my life — horses. They held me grounded to this earth when everything else flew away.

At nineteen, I was also running a large boarding and lesson stable with three other ladies. There were almost eighty horses on the farm. We had boarders, lesson horses, a trail-riding string, and a tack shop. It was there that I worked with my first children with special needs. One was a hearing-impaired girl who would ignore our mutually agreed-upon hand signals to change gait. When she wanted to keep cantering around the arena, she would look at the outside wall and avoid looking at me. What she learned quickly was that the horse was trained to verbal commands and would slide to a stop with a "Whoa!" It only took a time or two going from yeehaw to full stop before she went back to the mutually agreed-upon signals.

My second experience was with a girl who had ridden horses until she was in a car-versus-bicycle accident and lost her legs. We had to be very creative in finding a way to get her on the horse as we had no ramp or raised mounting areas. We found that the lift we stored jumps on worked well, and the horse was so patient and calm about the raising and lowering of the platform. This was my horse from childhood, and I had exposed him to so many things that he took it all in stride.

I moved on with my life to become a wife, mother, 4-H leader, librarian, and early childhood teacher, and I continued my journey to understand the creature that is the horse. I had some students during these years, and I always believed in working to make a connection with the horse rather than being the "master" of the horse.

My husband and I divorced after nineteen years of marriage, mainly because I didn't feel I needed to raise three teenagers (he being the third). Our two children were enough for me. Life was harder after that decision, yet more fulfilling, as I embarked on a journey to become someone other than his wife and the mother of his children. At that time, the only jobs I was qualified for were working with animals or children. The only jobs available in our area were with young (newborn to age five) children. I started working at a daycare as an infant caregiver for minimum wage. In many ways, that job changed my life forever. It started me down the path to working with kids with special needs in a profound way.

Also in that same year, I became aware of Sally Swift's way of thinking about rider and horse. I studied how the rider's position and body worked with — and sometimes against — the horse's natural way of going. I studied Pat Parelli's book *Natural Horse-Man-Ship: Six Keys to a Natural Horse-Human Relationship*. I was a student of that program for eight years and learned a lot about how horses think (according to Parelli) and how different personalities — horses' and humans' — may help or hinder that special bond between them.

My journey to become an early childhood teacher was a path of tossing out all the wrong information I had gathered during my life as a caregiver and mother. I absorbed the new information I wished I had had when my children were growing up. I learned about typical growth and development. I learned about meeting children where they were on that continuum. I also rediscovered how much

I enjoyed children. I especially enjoyed working with children who did not meet those typical expectations. I went on to build the first childcare center in our town. I owned and ran that childcare center for eight years until I ran out of steam.

After I sold the business, I worked for a friend who had one of the top in-home preschools in Madison, Wisconsin. Every year we had children with special needs. It was there that I met Jen Bluske, an occupational therapist and owner of Children's Therapy Network in Madison. I learned so much from watching her work with neurodivergent children. She was, and still is, an inspiration to me.

The twisting trail continued as my life veered off in another direction when I married my second husband, Dale — the love and best support person of my life. Amazingly, Dale believes in me and all my crazy ideas. We built That Zen Farm from bare fields of grass beginning in 1997 and have expanded and improved it ever since.

MY WHY

Even as a child, I was different — not neurodivergent, but different enough that I didn't quite fit in. My family called me the black sheep. For Christmas, they even bought me a black hoodie with a little jiggly bell on top so the "black sheep" wouldn't get lost. I didn't take offense, as it was true. I did not quite fit in with their boisterous ways. They loved to bicker and were always in motion. Their souls were young and full of adventure.

My parents were very young and wanted to stay that way, and my siblings were so much younger than I was that I became a caretaker instead of a playmate. When we moved to our farm, I found my place and my peace. I loved caring for the horses, the ducks, the goats, and the pet pig, Magnolia. The horses, though, were my other half. When I was with them, I could be quiet and calm. I could breathe in their peace and love.

At school I was a bit of an outsider, too. I liked people and enjoyed being around them, but I spent an inordinate amount of time talking about those lovely horses. I just couldn't help teaching everyone everything I knew. I'm sure I bored them to tears while I lived and breathed horses.

I loved being with kids, and I loved teaching. As a teenager, I took care of kids and taught riding lessons. Teaching filled me in ways that time with my family and peers never did. I loved helping people learn — and helping them laugh along the way. I spent more and more time with horses and friends who owned horses. I had no desire to be the type of girl my generation considered "normal." Because of past trauma, I didn't care about being the prettiest, the life of the party, or having a boyfriend. I didn't have any truly close girlfriends either. I drifted from one clique to another.

One group of girls, who were diligent students, became my favorites, as they weren't as judgmental as some of the others — perhaps because being a "smart girl" was also not very fashionable in high school. They folded me in, and many have remained part of my life ever since. I was terrible at makeup, fancy clothing, and flirting — skills that seemed to attract unwanted attention from boys. It was far easier for me to wrangle a thousand-pound horse with problems than wrestle with teenage-boy drama.

When I was younger, I wanted to be a horse trainer or a veterinarian. There weren't very many women in either of those careers during my young years. My parents and my loving grandparents spent a lot of time repeating that I couldn't make it as either of those. "There's no money in that," my grandma would say.

Unfortunately, I took that as the whole truth, and when I believed it, it did indeed become the truth. For years I trained horses and gave lessons and never made enough money to sustain myself. I went to university and let others around me convince me that girls couldn't get into veterinary school — that I wasn't smart enough, big enough, or competitive enough. I settled for running a stable, and I taught lessons at boarding places and then here on our farm. I never made enough money to live on. I felt I wasn't worthy of abundance.

In fact, those limiting beliefs followed me into all my entrepreneurial enterprises until I did my Gestalt work. I now know how good it feels to be worthy of love, abundance, and the knowledge I have gained through my life. Once I figured out who I was, I became who I was supposed to be. Everything, step by little step, led to where I am now.

What I learned was that I was always just a half-step out of rhythm with the rest of the world. I can empathize with the feeling of not fitting in, not knowing how to navigate social settings, and not having a large circle of friends. Eventually, I learned how to do those things, but it was a painful struggle. I had always been someone who felt things deeply — in my heart or in my gut. I had been trained to rely on logic, as emotions had no place in decision-making. Time and again, not trusting my heart and soul led to setbacks. Over time, I relearned to honor and trust those feelings.

I didn't know what was wrong with me, and it took tremendous effort to reach a place where I could expand my horizons. The EGCM program helped me find the real Marcy. Now, I help my clients understand who they are, find their own herd of supportive, loving friends, and walk in harmony with the world around them. Most importantly, I help them learn to love themselves. I want them to feel heard, recognized, and cherished for who they are in this place and time. My horses and I guide clients in discovering their true selves, setting their hearts on their visions, achieving their goals, and feeling whole.

CHAPTER TWO

MY PHILOSOPHY OF TEACHING

Be impeccable with your word
Don't take anything personally
Don't make assumptions
Always do your best

~ Don Miguel Ruiz, *The Four Agreements*

Teaching, for me, has never been a rigid set of rules or a one-size-fits-all method. It is a living practice — shaped by the children who arrive at the farm, the horses who partner with us, and the principles that guide how I show up in the world. Over the years, I've learned that true teaching begins long before a lesson plan and continues long after a session ends. It begins with presence, curiosity, and a willingness to meet each person exactly where they are. This chapter explores the foundations of that philosophy and the qualities that allow a teacher to support every learner with clarity, compassion, and respect.

START WHERE THE STUDENT IS

My teaching philosophy can be summed up in a simple statement: **Start where the student is and go from there**. Sounds simple enough, doesn't it? It can be when you understand child development, the level of understanding the child has, and the teacher's ability to read body language and facial expressions. I watch for tension in all parts of the body, especially the face. I feel for their fear or acceptance of being with the horse. I watch for changes in breathing and control of their core muscles. I'm looking for the utter delight in their eyes and the smile breaking out across their face.

It's part of the journey of a teacher to learn where to push and when to let go of an idea. Everyone has a point of no return. I have had to learn to see when frustration is turning from a motivator into a meltdown. If I'm not sure, I will err on the side of caution. I want every student to feel my empathy for their learning style and processing speed. I do not want them to associate being here on the farm with trauma. I want the farm to be a place of peace and learning.

We are called That Zen Farm for that very reason. I believe in my clients, at all ages and stages. I believe they can accomplish what they decide is best for them. I celebrate with them when they take each step and believe in themselves.

I believe we are all capable of learning at a pace that is uniquely our own. We all have the ability to solve problems in ways that reflect our individual strengths and rhythms. Most importantly, we are all whole, unique, and irreplaceable. Throughout my journey, I have embraced the ability to wholeheartedly integrate people into our unique program.

The ability to see both sides of an argument has gotten me into some interesting entanglements, and I've been called a fence sitter more than once. What those critics don't understand is that seeing both sides of a problem gives me an advantage. If I can get an inkling of how a person thinks — maybe even where they are coming from — I can assist them in seeing a bigger picture. Unfortunately, it doesn't seem to work where our national politics are concerned!

FIVE QUALITIES FOR TEACHERS WORKING WITH AUTISM SPECTRUM DISORDER (ASD)

There are five qualities that I feel make a great teacher: empathy, the ability to deconstruct tasks and goals into bite-size pieces, a rich vocabulary that allows the same concept to be explained in multiple ways, lots of patience, and a great sense of humor.

The first is **empathy**. Empathy is the foundation of teaching because it allows us to truly connect with students — to understand not only what they are learning but how they are experiencing the process. Without empathy, instruction becomes mechanical; with it, learning becomes human, supportive, and transformative. Yet empathy can be exhausting if I carry the weight of my own past trauma. Without clearing it, I risk burning out as I meet each client with compassion. Through the EGCM program, I was able to release that burden once and for all. This experience taught me how to feel, understand, and then let go of my clients' pain, allowing me to remain present and whole in their healing journey.

I completed the program to become a certified Equine Gestalt Coach, and to this day I continue to meet with my own coach when things get rough. My past no longer controls me, and I am able to sit in wholeness, listen deeply to another person's story, and help guide them toward discovering their own peace.

The second quality of a great teacher is the ability to **break tasks into small, manageable steps**, so each student can process them at their own pace. I adjust my teaching style to meet the learning style and pace of each individual. How much I break a task down depends on how the client processes information and their ability to remember the process. I explore this carefully and respectfully. If they can see the whole picture and accomplish the goal without my support, I say, "Yay!" Another may need each step added one by one and celebrated until the goal is achieved. I also had to learn which ones liked praise and which ones didn't. I find it fascinating that some don't need me to "pat them on the back" — they seem happy with their own sense of accomplishment.

The third quality of teaching is the ability to **explain the same concept in multiple ways**. I can explain how to post to the trot in many ways. My basic style of teaching is *Tell, Show, Do, Review.* This approach covers most learning styles. Auditory learners hear it, visual learners absorb the show, and kinesthetic learners need to do it. I love asking all my students what they learned that day. I get some hilarious answers. One child said she learned her pony was having a cranky day; another said his horse was acting like a teenager; and one said the horse was too bumpy!

The fourth quality of a great teacher is **patience** — with one's own frustrations, with the clients, and with the horses. I never allow myself to be frustrated with a student when they cannot figure out what I'm attempting to teach. I know it's my lack of communication skills that is causing the problem. I need to find the way that works for their mind to help them understand. If I can't get through with my usual bag of ideas, I go back to the drawing board and find a new way to say it or break it down. It's my responsibility to rectify the lack of comprehension.

I have noticed that the more I work with kids who are literal thinkers, the more my own language has had to become clearer and more precise. I use fewer words and explanations, offering simplicity first. When they question "why," then I allow myself to expand and provide more detail. As a preschool teacher, I heard "why" so many times I became desensitized to it. Over time, I have learned to turn the question back to them, inviting them to explore their own reasoning and share what they thought the "why" might be behind a certain activity.

Not surprisingly, little folks are brilliant observers and have creative minds — as do my autistic spectrum clients. They seem to NEED to know ALL. It seems to be part of their communication system that works for them. When they know it all, they can carry on a conversation with another person because they have all the facts. For me, they are learning, and I love it when that happens.

My partners, the horses, know a lot about what is needed — often before I do. They are great teachers. As individuals, they also have different personalities. Naughty John (a Haflinger) may bond more easily with a child than Nein (John's half-brother). The Rose (an Arabian mare) may be ticklish and require a different brush or different pressure. Billy Bob (another Haflinger) loves hard rubbing to get all his itchy spots.

The client is asked to pay attention to what the horse is saying to them. The horse may pick up on the child's energy hum and either stay super calm or join in the energy. I help each person — children and adults alike — understand what they are seeing and assist them in learning how to be a better partner to the horse who wants to be with them. My goal is to build a connection to the horse first through respectful interaction and then build trust and partnership.

The fifth quality for being a great teacher and coach is to **find your sense of humor**! I have become an expert on sarcasm, slapstick, silliness, puns, and all-out laughing out loud. The jokes are never about the person and always about something that can't be hurt by what is being said. That's hard to achieve with sarcasm, but it can be done with a little work. Laughter dissipates anxiety and fear — it relaxes and it bonds. I work hard to find what kind of humor brings a smile or a laugh from my clients. Humor helps my day be better too.

CHAPTER THREE

AUTISM AND ASD

"The only disability in life is a bad attitude."

~ Scott Hamilton

While I am not an expert in this field, I have had experience working with all ages of people diagnosed with ASD for more than twenty-five years. A good deal of my amazing clientele has this diagnosis. I see them in both my Energy Connected Therapeutic Horsemanship sessions and in my EGCM practice.

WHAT IS ASD?

Autism spectrum disorder begins in early childhood, often within the first year. It is currently thought to be genetic (which usually means one or both parents are on the spectrum). As a spectrum disorder, it can manifest in so many ways that it's hard to pin down what I see. ASD is highly individualistic. The best I can say is that I see some general similarities and lots of things that are unique to the individual. The usual traits neurotypical people think of are an inability to read social cues, lack of eye contact, difficulty communicating, poor muscle tone, and unregulated behaviors. The social difficulties often lead to masking, which — while useful for a while (even years) — can eventually cause a great deal of psychological distress and burnout.

At one end of the spectrum is a fully functional individual with some social-connection difficulties; at the other is someone who is nonverbal, combative, extremely low-toned, and highly sensitive to all things sensory (light, sound, physical touch).

A new young client came to us with multiple health issues, nonverbal, severe epilepsy corrected with surgery but still very far behind in development, and more than a bit afraid of the new thing that smelled funny and was huge. We worked on touching, then brushing. When I said she needed to wear a helmet before she could ride, her parents were skeptical, as she fought against wearing one even for her bicycle. They said they would work through it at home. The next week, they arrived with her wearing the bike helmet. I rarely allow it, but I knew we would be going slowly with the safest horse on the farm. We went through all the stages of preparation. She was definitely ready to step into the saddle. With a little encouragement, she climbed up for that first magical ride. After that day, she would come to her parents with her helmet in her hands and indicate that she wanted to ride again. She is amazing.

When I was new to the early childhood field, physicians were very reluctant to diagnose young children and preferred parents wait until the child started school. We, as teachers of the very young, could see the child needed help. Birth-to-three services came into our world, and we have had some success in their application in working with the young children. Sometimes the parents struggled with accepting that their child needed help.

Thirty years later, I see more services provided at a younger age and better outcomes than in the past. Public education has also helped. Even with that, it is hard for parents of neurotypical children to understand the depth and breadth of the autism spectrum. It's hard to see what strength it takes to be a child who has no control at times, who cannot connect, and in some cases cannot even communicate. What I work with now are some of those children who didn't get help when they were little. I have also seen children who received services at a young age. I'm inspired by how they have learned to be who they truly are, which is so awesome to me.

I also have clients who were not given an autism diagnosis until they were adults. My job is to find a way to connect with them and bring forth whatever I can to help them find joy in being with the horse. For me, getting a diagnosis is important so they can receive help that is often long overdue. I'm not a fan of labels. When they come here, I drop the label and find the person within. The older my client is when they receive a diagnosis, the harder it seems to be on them — at least for those who come here for help. I am seeing more and more adults getting diagnoses of attention deficit hyperactivity disorder (ADHD) attention deficit disorder (ADD), and ASD. It seems to be a shock to their system, even though they know they've had difficulties all their lives. The horses and I work with them to understand who they are now and find their path.

The joy they find with the horse has little to do with me and everything to do with the horse. Horses have an amazing capacity for love and sharing their vibrational energy. I can't explain it, as science hasn't quite caught up with the proof of it, but I know it happens. Children who have never smiled before beam their joy at being with the horse. The sweetest sight for me is a person who buries their nose in the horse's coat and breathes in the scent deeply.

WHAT DOES ALL THIS HORSE BUSINESS HAVE TO DO WITH HELPING ASD CLIENTS (AND OTHERS)?

A study done in 2015 with 127 ASD children, led by Robin Gabriels in conjunction with the Autism Research Institute, showed improvements in irritability and hyperactivity as well as increased word fluency when working with horses. Six months later, the children continued to exhibit reductions in irritability compared to controls. They also maintained their social communication and word fluency. Robin Gabriels commented that there is growing evidence that they can improve through work with horses.[1]

In a totally unscientific survey of the parents of the children I work with, the results were interesting and as varied as the children themselves. The parents noted physical improvements such as focus, better walking skills, balance, success at horse riding, and core strength.

One of my main goals is to help my clients learn to self-regulate. When a client is with a horse, they need emotional as well as physical control over themselves. Understanding how the horse responds to their emotional energy, and even their physical energy, helps them understand what they are feeling, which can be confusing for ASD kids and adults alike. Horses may mirror what we give them. If the rider is afraid, the horse will sense that and be less responsive. If the rider believes in the next movement around the arena or on a trail, the horse will mirror that back too. In this way, horses help these clients understand the complex web of emotions their nervous system is feeling in the moment. They need the awareness to know when they are losing that control. When they want to be with the horse and work toward a beautiful partnership, it opens the doors to self-regulation. While this takes a while to master when away from the horse, most work hard at it when they are here. Parents report that the children go home very calm and at peace.

Others noted gains in compassion, learning how to communicate with another species, and a loss of fear around horses. For me, the most important part changes to observe were the internal emotional shifts that have emerged. Parents and children have noticed growth

---

[1] Robin L. Gabriels et al., "Randomized Controlled Trial of Therapeutic Horseback Riding in Children and Adolescents With Autism Spectrum Disorder," *Journal of the American Academy of Child & Adolescent Psychiatry* 54, no. 7 (2015): 541-549; summarized in "Horse Therapy Benefits for Autism," Autism Research Institute, and David Kelly, "Children with Autism Spectrum See Benefits from Equine Therapy," University of Colorado Anschutz Medical Campus press release.

in self-awareness and self-respect, along with increased confidence and an improved ability to read body language. Children say that they trust the horse, as well as the teachers and volunteers, and that they feel calmer — their anxiety is quieted while here and, for some, throughout the week in between.

In the neurotypical children, the answers were much the same, with the addition of learning patience, animal care, decision-making, finding their voice, and leadership.

SUCCESS

What does success look like? Success is any time a client overcomes whatever is causing a block to learning. For some, it may be as simple as standing in the arena with a horse. When that happens, we have success number one and celebrate at whatever level is appropriate for that client.

For others, it's the first time they can put the saddle on without assistance. Later, it may be riding independently or bringing the horse in from the pasture (with a volunteer). The sky's the limit. Celebrating may be as quiet as a thumbs-up or as jubilant as jumping around. Everything is tailored to the needs of the client and where they are in their own process.

In adult clients, my work entails assisting them to find who they are. The conversations and journey are more nuanced than with some of the children, but I have found that adults who are diagnosed later in life have difficulty seeing who they truly are. They have faked it until they are no longer capable of doing so. I see the devastation of this crash, the confusion of receiving a diagnosis of autism, ADHD, ADD, or OCD (obsessive compulsive disorder) — diagnoses they may never have imagined they would have. I usually spend a lot of time listening to these adults as they process what is weighing on them.

WALKING AWAY

I firmly believe that all people have good and bad days, and we at That Zen Farm are a judgment-free zone. I haven't walked away from any of them. Some have walked away from me because of my sticking to my code of conduct with horses and humans. Some people don't understand my empathy for horses and for humans. We firmly believe that taking the time it takes, rather than pushing, is the path to follow. The horse is a partner in this business, and if they don't like what is going on in the rider's body, the horse's discomfort will be listened to. Most of the time, the break is because they don't understand the horse and what pressure does to them and won't believe or want to understand that I will put the horse first. While they are advocating for their children, I advocate for my herd.

I never harbor unhealthy feelings for people when they leave, and sometimes they come back. I lay down the rules quickly. If I see a person (child or adult) handling a horse roughly — patting them hard, running at them, or yelling at them — I stop them and explain the rules. It is then up to them whether they stay and learn a better way or move on to another place.

TALKING WITH THE PARENTS

I respect the parents of my clients. They know their child better than anyone on the planet. I ask them to watch for signs that we have pushed far enough and to let me know. I ask them about behaviors I should be aware of to keep the child safe and regulated. I speak loudly enough, when the child's sensory limits allow, that the parent can hear what I am saying. I explain what I am doing and my goals for their child. I tell them that it takes the time it takes, and we are not in a hurry. I want to build trust between the child and horse, the child and teachers, and parents and teachers. One of the key ingredients is listening deeply when the client or the parent is speaking, honoring what they feel, and assisting them in seeing another point of view.

When I have adult clients who come with one or both parents, we spend time talking about expectations and goals. I am focused on the client, and if the client is comfortable with parents listening, they are allowed to stay. Hopefully, I'm modeling asking open-ended questions and listening deeply to my client. Parents have spent the child's life putting out fires, advocating, and fighting for the child's rights. I model paying attention to what the client is saying so that I can assist them in using their knowledge and applying it to the rules of social norms, dealing with people, and dealing with frustrations.

Adult clients who arrive on their own are treated as welcomed guests who are seeking solutions. My job, as always, is to facilitate problem-solving and trauma release through the Gestalt techniques that I spent four years absorbing.

ARRIVING AT THE FARM

The drive from any of the neighboring towns and cities is calming and full of rural beauty — rolling hills, farms, cows, horses, and vistas all around. Pulling onto our driveway, you will find a fruit-tree-lined drive with horse pastures on each side. As you pass the barn, you see a parking lot facing the Swiss-chalet-style home on the hill. It too is flanked by horses. The nearby henhouses are filled with busy hens searching for bugs and clucking contentedly, and the roosters crow as you exit the car. The atmosphere is calm and peaceful. There are two large red buildings: the first is a barn with horse stalls and stacks of hay; the second is the riding arena. The arena doors are open and inviting, with irises blooming in the summertime to welcome visitors.

After visiting the farm, Cameron Lee Cowan, who helped bring this book to life, wrote: "Like many farms, there are old cars rusting away amid tall grasses, a variety of fences to keep animals in, and pathways leading to buildings. The property is sheltered by trees which separate it from the road and the fields around it. It feels like a secret." His description was so accurate that I had to include his unique (and autistic) perspective.

A small stone Zen garden leads to the entry for people. Everyone is gently and calmly greeted and led inside where the magic happens. The horses who will be working are usually in the arena awaiting the clients.

WORKING WITH LATE-DIAGNOSED AUTISM

"I'm not weird, I'm wired differently."

~ Erin Geddes

Apparently, the universe has planned for me to work with all ages of neurodivergent people. I have the greatest admiration for those who have spent a lifetime mirroring the people around them just to get through the day. One man told me that he would go home, take off the mask, and fall apart. He thought everyone did that. Wearing a "mask" was his way to deal with the "I don't really know how I'm supposed to act and do this work, play, interactions, but everyone else is doing this thing and so I will do it like them."

When he returned home from a day of work, he would remove that strangeness and become himself, usually exhausted from being someone who was not his true self. He was quite successful at mirroring and being a productive person. He said the playacting could only be sustained for so long, and then he crashed. By his mid-forties, his mental health became unstable enough that he fell apart and sought help. When he was diagnosed with ASD and other mental-health diagnoses, it was the first time in his life he understood that he was neurodivergent. Then the questions began to plague him: *Where do I go? What am I capable of doing now? And who the hell am I now?*

When they come here, I listen. I have found that listening may be my greatest gift to them. The shock of discovering they are not the people they thought they were is a huge burden. They must learn a whole new set of rules and a new way of being because they can't go back to the mask and mirroring. I often see grief, sadness, anger, and frustration.

Our work together brings those emotions to light so they can be worked through and put to rest. The horses often move in to touch the person on the heart or lower back and hold space while I listen. Often the client feels the need to stand and touch the horse in return. I work to heal the connection between who they thought they were and who they truly are. It can be a long process of release, acceptance, and rebuilding. We set goals and create a vision of their future, then create plans of action to get there. Success is when the client decides they know who they are and where they want to be and what they want to do.

One of my clients had been living at home, and it was not a stable environment for him to grow and thrive. We worked on what it would look like if he lived in a group home or on his own. We worked on his self-awareness, self-compassion, forgiveness, and life goals, and created a vision board. He has lofty goals: becoming a martial-arts actor, writing an epic heroic tale, and finding a girlfriend. If you can dream, you can achieve. We set goals, worked with his case manager, and he visited group homes, visited martial-arts studios near the homes, looked for jobs, interviewed, and got a job. Now he is happy, working hard, back in martial-arts classes, and at last contact he was staying mentally healthy.

It looks different for each client based on their needs and dreams. They may be able to go back to school, hold a full-time job, be calm when they never thought they could, and still be themselves. They can see the person they always wanted to be.

Success may be the ability to be at ease with life as it is right now. The goal is the client's own. While I may see more for their lives than they can see, I can wait until they get there. A lifetime of being out of step takes a while to catch up — if that's what they want. It is up to them.

I do work with teenagers who cannot cope with the stress of public school. They are lost too — they need contact with peers, yet are unable to make good decisions or understand social rules. Sometimes the system lets them down, and sometimes they let themselves down. Either way, we work together to seek a path they are capable of walking to achieve a goal.

Unfortunately, many are homeschooling, and instead of doing their work, they spend their time playing games online or browsing social media. They often isolate themselves from their families to avoid conflict, which only makes their problems worse. Many struggle to look beyond each day and have difficulty seeing a future. I spend a great deal of time growing their trust in me through the horses. Once trust is built with the horse, then they slowly begin talking to me. I work to assist them in expanding their world. We work to find a vision and a way to achieve that goal. I help them find connection to their emotions. They often don't recognize or have words for hope, empathy, and sympathy. And we work to find the words to speak their truth, to respond rather than react.

I have been working with a young man named Trevor for the past four years. He started with me while still in high school and has a background of mental-health issues as well as ASD. This past year, since graduating, he has been working toward finding a job and exploring the possibility of attending community college. He is quite anxious about all of that. We've been working on social skills in the workplace, including how peer expectations may differ from those of the employer.

I found through listening deeply that we shared a favorite author, Anne McCaffrey, and her world of dragons on the planet Pern. It was a great starting point to compare McCaffrey's view on society, Trevor's view, and mine. It led to some very interesting discussions and some sticking points. Staying in the bedroom playing games with "friends" who are only known through online gaming is his safe zone. Opening his mind to the fact that it can be safe outside those walls has been a challenge.

I'm always creating ways to break through the walls Trevor has built to protect himself from the world. Recently, one of my beloved ponies died of kidney failure at the age of twenty-one. I was devastated, as Naughty John had been with me since he was a year old — an amazing fellow with a heart of gold. I asked Trevor if I could assist him with his listening skills, as I had noticed that he often interrupted when someone else wanted to talk. He immediately apologized, and I replied that there was a certain awareness to listening that people don't often think about. I explained that we often listen to reply and don't fully hear what the other person is saying. He agreed to listen quietly and to give me feedback about what he heard when I was finished.

I told him the story of Naughty John. I started with when we first met and how he came home and grew into a sweet, funny, top-notch escape artist. I told him about John's work with children with special needs, his illness, the frustration of diagnosing and treating that illness, and finally, his death.

I was choking up with tears. Trevor got up from his chair, grabbed a few tissues, bent down, and hugged me as I finished the story. He held me while I cried and said, "You nearly had me in tears too. I'm sorry John died."

I rejoiced for him. This young man, who had been known for his angry reactions, had listened well, empathized, and sympathized with my pain. It is always my mission to assist my clients in finding self-awareness and self-compassion. Trevor also grew into awareness of others and compassion for them as well. And Naughty John added one more magical story to his legacy.

CHAPTER FOUR

EQUINE GESTALT COACHING

In South Africa, the northern Natal tribe has a greeting, *Sawa bona*. It means "I see you" in the most literal way. The reply offered is *Sikhona*. It means "I am here."

Many years ago, I realized that there was more to horses than riding, or being used as a teaching tool, and even more than being best friends. For years, I searched for the niche that suited my unique view of the world. I have always strived to make a difference in people's lives and lead with compassion. Where was that elusive spot in the horse world for my horses and me?

HISTORY

When I was young, there was limited access to any kind of therapy for children. Even if my parents had noticed that something was different about me, they would have had nowhere to take me. I now understand that they were probably so absorbed in their own search for maturity that, because I was quiet and obedient, they assumed I was doing fine.

At the age of six, I was taking on the role of caregiver for my siblings and my parents. Even when I was sexually assaulted at thirteen, I told no one, and no one noticed. It never crossed my mind to enter therapy as an adult. There was, in my mind at least, a stigma around that. I was coping after all. I was doing well. No need for extra help here — or so I thought.

What I did learn to do was listen: to children who were under my care, to animals, and to friends who needed a sympathetic and empathetic ear. I helped where I could and sympathized where I could not.

I searched for a career where these values could assist others in their journeys. I looked at many different models, and the only one that resonated with me was the EGCM program. It had horses, who are natural masters of Gestalt and living in the moment, Gestalt methodology, and coaching others to find a wholeness of self.

In life, there are times when you meet angels on earth. I have met many since I started the EGCM certification program in 2019. The first one I met was Melisa Pearce — the founder, teacher, advisor, and angel of the program. I didn't know the trauma I had endured and pushed deep down inside as a youngster was going to need to be dealt with. She knew long before I knew myself. There was work to be done. Thankfully, she accepted me into the program.

I was sixty-five years old, and I had no idea what it all entailed! It would be two years of hard study learning about areas of life I had never experienced. It had been twenty-five years since I had put my nose to the grindstone to get homework done, and I had to learn how to use Zoom and work online. At home, I was still running the riding lesson program and helping on the farm. Most frightening of all was the travel. Suddenly my life was filled with planes, trains, automobiles, motels, and altitude sickness. I had hardly left the farm and its nearby towns for years.

I spent the next two years finding out who I was under the layers of tamped-down trauma. Two years of discovering that I am worthy of love and abundance (not just monetarily). I had to stretch and seek the drive to learn a new language and revisit emotional connections with people I had packed away. At least I knew horses — or so I thought! I had always had a deep connection with my horses. We had been teaching kids with special needs for twenty years at that point. I had so much to learn about what horses could do beyond my current understanding and expectations.

I felt a nervous ball of queasiness settle in my stomach when I learned I would have to be in a group of women for each CORE (the intensive in-person training in Colorado) four times a year. I was about to take a chance with women I had never met. They would hear my deep secrets and pain. I gambled that this was my best chance to fulfill that elusive dream I had of assisting others. Those first two years taught me to appreciate women as loving, empathic, and giving friends. I had rarely had that deep kind of friendship with women. I observed women with terrible trauma become healers of the highest quality and supreme light workers. These women showed me in our first meeting how to reach forward and deal with their trauma and then reach back and help others up.

One woman I met early in my CORE training showed me that even when growing up with a horrendous and unstable mother, it is possible to heal from those wounds and not only serve as a great lawyer but also become an extraordinary healer. Hers is a journey of courage and triumph. She had made a tremendous spiritual journey of her own and tucked me beneath her strong and comforting arm when I began my journey into the world of finding my own spirituality and acceptance of ideas I had been trained to ridicule and dismiss. Her story is told in *Alchemy of Resistance: My Rugged Path to Wholeness* by Hertha Lund.

To my amazement, there were a few men in the program, and they were excellent at this work. They were kind, caring, and gentle. I didn't know if I could speak of my own trauma with men in the room, and yet I felt safe and heard. Their gentle energy was a first step forward in my journey to lose my fear of men. They wiped clean some relentless negative opinions I had carried for a lifetime. I heartily thank them for that. Without their help, I would not be as successful at coaching men as I am now.

I had lost trust in men — except for my husband Dale. Early in our relationship, he had shown me that he could be trusted and that it was safe to speak what was on my heart and mind. Dale possesses an inner peace that radiates from him — a soft, calm energy that is unflappable. He can get angry, but he manages it within a reasonable frame. I hadn't experienced that before in a man.

I found that opening myself to new friendships and allowing myself to trust that there are more people who care expanded my own compassion and understanding. I also find it interesting that I need to switch gears when going from working with a woman to working with a man.

My perception is that women want face-to-face conversations and empathetic dialogue. The men seem more comfortable when our chairs are side by side or at least angled toward each other. Most of the men I work with like to start with the logical thinking side of their brains and wait until they are comfortable with me before delving into how they feel about a memory or life situation. Without the superb coaching I received during the four years of Gestaltist certification training, I wouldn't be the knowledgeable, flexible coach that I am today.

I had found my herd. They believed that everyone deserves to be the best they can be, and they all loved horses. When I entered the program, I thought I was simply adding to and expanding my current level of knowledge. It was so much more than that. It changed the course of my life. Things I had held onto with mistaken fervor were released, and my inner self was transformed.

I am now grounded, at peace, and have self-awareness and self-compassion. I can love myself as much as I love and care for others.

I opened my heart and let the Gestalt work unlock and unchain the trunks of pain hidden deep inside me. They were the things that held me back from my authenticity. I had been hiding my innate self under a basket created by the adults around me when I was young.

When I entered the program, I was feeling and understanding the energy of my horses and using it as a focus to train them. Even then, I hid from the deeper messages they were asking me to receive. I had blocked most people's energy except to keep myself safe and to teach. I was protecting myself and missing so many pieces needed to assist others in finding their authenticity.

Gestalt helped me understand and accept the good and profound release of trauma. Accepting meant I had to find a way to understand the source of my fear, anger, and emotional brick walls. I had to learn to release it to become whole.

My first hard lesson was to accept that my client's problems weren't mine to take in and solve. I had no right to their pain or any reason to believe I had the answer for them. That's their job. I had to learn how to ask the right questions to assist them in understanding and rewiring their own brains to accept and see their own path to wholeness.

I had closed off the energy of other people — a shield was in place to keep their emotional vibrations from affecting me. Once I dealt with my own trauma and put it to rest, I could sit with those who struggle with their own waves of trauma and emotions. Now their emotions flow through me without pain or judgment, acknowledged and understood as their journey and not my own. I work with my clients to find ways that they too can cope with vibrational energy — their own or that which is coming from others.

Equine Gestalt coaching is a partnership between coach, horse, and client to assist the client in finding self-awareness and self-compassion, and also to resolve past trauma. As Gestaltists, we believe that people are whole, capable, and resourceful in solving their own problems. I ask the questions and encourage them to find their true path — the road that's right for them.

The first group session (CORE) I attended in Colorado was where we took our first steps to become coaches and began resolving our own issues within ourselves. A young woman did a piece of work with Melisa, and something in the work set off fears, alarms, and a deep panic inside me. When Melisa called for anyone who felt they needed work done, I timidly raised my hand.

I could feel that Melisa knew exactly what needed to be opened. I didn't even know that my mind had buried the trauma ten feet deep — the trauma from when I was six years old and that pedophile had twisted me into his toy. It only ended when he died when I was about eight years old. I had held that trauma for my whole life, pushing it down and away, especially when the emotional pain would send warnings through my body. When the piece of work was finished, I was free of that deep burden. I discovered the gift of that trauma was that I took on the role of guardian of children. That role has led to almost all the jobs I have had in my life: caregiver, horsemanship teacher, mother, children's librarian, early childhood teacher, special-needs horsemanship teacher, and now Equine Gestalt Coach. All these previous "jobs" led me to becoming a Gestaltist.

Once I became aware of walls and blockages in my body, I was on a mission to fix them. In the past, I would feel scary emotions and block them from coming into full recognition. I now allow the feelings to flow through me, and I stand with empathy and energy for myself and the client.

Every time we had a group meeting in Colorado, I would learn more about myself — about things that had been buried and only raised their ugly heads occasionally. I thought I was handling those events — I was wrong again. When I was sexually assaulted and shoved it down deep inside, I thought I was fine. I could carry on;

I could have intimate relationships with men. I could — but not really, and not in true intimacy. All my relationships failed, because the moment they became too intimate, I was out of there and would end the relationship.

I continued that pattern of avoiding intimacy until I met my first husband. I told him about it and how my parents didn't believe me. He decided he would be the one to teach me what physical love was all about — and he certainly did. Unfortunately, that was his only love language, and that language lacked emotional connection and intimacy in other ways I didn't even know I was missing. For him, love was sex and sex was love.

After nineteen years, we divorced. His lack of true and intimate love, self-centeredness, and alcoholism tore us apart. We have two wonderful children, and for that I am forever grateful. What I didn't know was that if I had released the terror and the anger from the rape before we met, I would have been a different person. I may also have walked away before becoming involved with him at all.

One of the brightest parts of my journey was my spiritual journey. It's not part of the program, but it was part of my journey to find myself. Having grown up in an atheist household, I was adrift in my spiritual journey. My parents allowed me to explore churches and other religions even as they scoffed at it. When I attended each church, I left with the feeling of being inherently bad and that churches wanted my money. I was neither bad nor did I have money, so I stopped attending any church. I tried fourteen different churches before I was fourteen years old. They left a bitter taste in my soul. I found I was empty and had little faith in anything.

During one of the CORE sessions I attended, I did a huge piece of work on releasing the anger from being sexually assaulted. I hated the man who did it, and that felt wrong. It was against my true self and was hard to live with. After the Gestalt work, I felt there was a hole in my center. I sat with it all night and wondered what to do with it. I couldn't walk around like that, could I? The next day we were working in teams on metaphors.

Perfect. I felt like I was standing at the rim of this abyss, and I was going to fall in and be lost forever. As we worked through the metaphor, I began to see pulsing balls of light — a blue one, a green one, a red one, and many other colors — coming toward me and encircling me. Suddenly, a golden light poured over me from above. I felt utterly and completely calm and free of anxiety. As the light settled in around me, I saw two figures above my right shoulder. One was as beautifully angelic as any artist would have portrayed, and the other an elder male dressed in monk-like garb. The names Gabriel and Francis came to me. I cannot explain to you what this was all about. I had no idea. What did I know about angels?

So now what do I do with two angels hanging over my right shoulder? I had learned that Gabriel was the messenger of God. I could hardly say the word "God," let alone believe I was touched by his messenger. I was going to have to stew about this. Hertha Lund, a fellow student a year ahead of me, offered me her insights. She is the most highly spiritual person I have ever met. She was able to answer some of my questions.

Melisa too had ideas and concepts for me that were mind-blowing. I settled into the idea of having angels on my shoulder, as they didn't seem to want to go. I went with the flow, and I thanked them every night before sleeping. I only ask for help protecting our horses, family, farm, and friends when it might be needed. I'm not sure about the rules yet.

A couple of CORE sessions later, I experienced another spiritual journey. As students of Equine Gestalt coaching, we are encouraged to resolve the trauma we have pushed down in our lives and be at peace. Part of my journey was as a seeker of spirituality. I needed answers before I could move on to being whole and a healer. I dug into my soul and found I was not good enough, unseen, unheard for most of my life. And I was unworthy. Asking for help was one of the hardest things to do on this journey. I gave in and asked.

I discovered that my rejection of the churches and "all things God" had hurt my soul. I touched on other beliefs and alternative thoughts. Nothing held my attention for long. I buried all of that and went on with my life. It was time to unbury, unlock, and open that old trunk to fully heal. I needed faith in something to be whole. I needed to be a light worker, and I needed to understand in my soul what light is. I found myself talking to the angels. I still could not say the word "God." It stuck in my throat like a lump. But I talked, and I questioned, and I cried. Then I went to the top of the mounting block and answered those same questions in the voice of the angels that surrounded me. This was the key that opened me to feeling loved, heard, and enough. I am still on the journey and still have trouble saying the word "God." For now, I call this place of peace, love, and healing a place of angels. I do fully understand that what I feel is love — and that I am worthy of that love. This is my journey to find what I believe and who I am.

THE POWER OF VALUES

One of the important parts of figuring out who I was and where I wanted to go was learning my values. My values drive my decisions, and my decisions guide my destiny. We were required to figure out what our values were and how we lived by them. I never thought the exercise would be so arduous. It was a struggle to understand what drove me, what I would accept in my life, and what I absolutely would not. What did I base my decisions on?

It took several months to discover the obvious: **compassion ruled my every decision**. My love and care for children and animals raised me as much as I raised them, and it filled me to care for others. For me, compassion is about love, caring, empathy, sympathy, and sometimes a gentle nudge to help someone find the answers for themselves. I had to acknowledge that some people viewed my compassion as a weakness — and I disagree. When I give from the heart, I receive as much or more back. How can that be a weakness? I feel it's my greatest strength.

My second value is that I strive to make a difference in people's lives by being a patient teacher and a compassionate coach. I have placed myself as a lifelong learner. Recently, I discovered a new value I had never considered before: **the gift of service to others**. Before entering the Equine Gestalt coaching program, I had a different definition of the word "service." I defined service as police, firefighters, EMTs, paramedics, and the military. Now I feel that what I do is also serving the world, even if it is only my small corner of it.

What I have learned since graduating is that I am indeed in service to those who come here to our farm. My desire is to assist people in discovering who they truly are, learning to love themselves, and releasing past trauma.

BEING ANGRY AND "MOVE AWAY" VALUES

One of my most valued lessons during the four years of EGCM training at Touched By A Horse was discovering my move away values. I will do anything to avoid being angry, frustrated, or fearful. I am generally a happy, grounded, and loving person.

Recently, those values were sorely tested. We went through a weekend that shook my calm foundation to the core. The whole thing deeply troubled me. I had a hard time turning the events around to a good viewpoint and way of thinking.

We have a neighbor — identity unknown, somewhere "over there" — who likes to shoot rapid-fire gun rounds. We live far out in the country, and the horses are used to the trap-shooting club behind us, so they mostly ignore the sounds. However, on this particular Saturday, the neighbor decided to throw in a new element: Tannerite bombs! Tannerite is legal here, but boy, are they LOUD! You can load them into a refrigerator and explode them so the sound becomes cannon-like. I don't know what they loaded up to explode, but it shook my indoor arena — and me too.

Most weekends, I have back-to-back lessons with special-needs children. The horses need to be cool, calm, and connected (not collected). My staff member and I were working with two new horses and didn't have any children on horseback when the arena shook. The horses were wary but not overly frightened. We decided for the rest of the day to work only on the ground and keep things as safe as possible. A short while later we had Nein in the arena — he grew up with the trap shooting — when another BOOM went off. He was terribly shaken, wide-eyed, and tense. We had to pull him from the line-up for the rest of the day. His fear spread to the other horses who were waiting for their turn to teach.

The noises went on all afternoon. *Pow! Pow! Pow! Pow! BOOM!* Even the horses in the pastures were scared and running in all directions. We decided to keep the children on the ground instead of riding. It took a lot of constant grounding and centering from the teachers to keep everyone on an even keel.

The next morning, I brought two of my usual ponies into the arena. Nein had been with us a long time but was fairly new to the lesson program. We could see that he was still a bit unnerved by the noise event from the day before. It was windy, but no Tannerite was going off. His nervousness escalated, and then his brother, John, started reacting to the atmosphere. John has always been a steady-eddy, but he was rattled by the energy that Nein was producing. Then two cats had an altercation, and Nein was done. He couldn't focus and was startled by every little sound. John went sideways when Nein did and sent his rider onto the sand on her behind. This child had been with me for eight years, and it was the first time she had fallen off. She was unhurt but a little afraid to get back on. We problem-solved together whether it was a good idea to get back on. She felt she should and climbed back on. John was still on guard but did not spook. She walked him once around and got down calmly and gently.

I cancelled the rest of the classes for the day. It isn't worth the chance of a child getting hurt or a horse reacting in fear. Fear is an education killer — a person can't learn if they are afraid, and neither can a horse.

I was absolutely furious with the person who thought it was fun to blow up Tannerite. Their fun and games messed up my horses' confidence, my riders' safety, and my income source. My own emotional health was suffering too. And those folks had no clue. I stewed for the rest of the weekend. I was at a loss over what to do next. I had missed the opportunity to call the sheriff's department; I didn't know where the sound came from; and I was a little worried about sending someone out looking for the noisy neighbors. I added a little anger at myself into the mix.

The next day I had to go into town. As I was driving home, a sheriff's deputy was coming in. I flagged him down, and he pulled over and came to my truck window. I explained what we heard and the trouble it caused. He told me about Tannerite and that it was legal. He also said I could call in a noise complaint, and they would go and find the source. He mentioned that often the people doing this have no idea what consequences their actions have on those around them.

I felt the anger slip away. I had told my story and was heard. And I had an action plan for next time.

It took several days for Nein to be calm enough to ride again. Several months later, he is still a bit cautious in the arena. We hope that time — and no repeats of the problem — will assist him in relaxing fully. We hope that his love of children will bring back his confidence.

FINDING GRIT AND GRACE

I had to learn to stop listening to the voices from my childhood that repeated I couldn't be a veterinarian because I was a girl, that horses were money pits, and that there was no future in them. I was molded uncomfortably into becoming what girls of my generation were expected to be: a mother and homemaker. I was told to be quiet and listen to my elders. I stayed silent too long. It was a long road to find my voice and my niche.

I learned so much more than Gestalt methodology in those first two years of study. I learned about business practices far beyond what I had picked up in all my other entrepreneurial attempts. I learned about facilitating groups and building a database. I awakened the skills to touch the inner energy of both humans and horses — skills I had as a child but lost along the way. In that awakening, my other business began to bloom as well. Many of my special-needs clients cannot understand, regulate, or express how they are feeling. I am more aware of what they are feeling now and can assist them in finding a way to express themselves in a positive way.

What I learned most was how amazing my horse partners were. I knew as a teenager that my horses were my salvation — my shield against a complex and sometimes unfair, cruel world. What I didn't know was how deep their work on me went. The way they work with people and what they show me about the client is so mind-blowing that at first I wasn't sure it was really happening. The more I work in this field, the more humble and grateful I am for their partnership.

I had no way of knowing that my past affected my present and future. One of my biggest moments was realizing that the truth — that I *could* be successful in a career with horses — had always been within my grasp, once I let go of the limiting beliefs that were holding me back.

THE FIRST EQUINE GESTALT COACHING CLIENTS

I gained such confidence in what I was about to embark upon that my first clients were mental-health patients enrolled in a special program that allowed them to choose what therapies and coaching they thought would be helpful for them. I became a provider through the help of Melisa Pearce's recommendation, and through the head of the department who saw something in this coaching modality with horses that would be good for her clients — even though I didn't have a degree in anything. I called Melisa before the first clients arrived. Was I ready for clients who were diagnosed with mental-health issues?

Was I scared that I would let them down? You bet. I knew my clients were a bit more fragile than someone who came through the public access. I knew I had to take my time and earn their trust. I found the grounding, self-confidence, and deep-listening skills I needed to assist them in finding themselves. Once a client stepped into my sacred and safe place of healing, I was one hundred percent the Equine Gestaltist and fully present in my authentic self.

The big draw for many of my clients is simply the fact that they will be near horses. They know they won't be riding, and some have never even been near a horse before, but they feel drawn to them. Of course, we always begin with a safety demonstration to keep everyone safe.

What surprises even the ones who have ridden or owned horses is the depth at which the horses give me clues about what is going on inside of them. A change of breath in the client or the horse after the client speaks, a horsey nose pressed gently against a part of the client's body, a nudge, or a leaching (a type of yawning) from the horse — all of these tell a story about what is happening internally. My job is to ask the right questions so the client can also see what might be going on inside and release that trauma.

For some, the work is fun and interesting, and they dive right into the experiential process. For others, it feels so emotionally charged that they want to back away. I meet them at whatever level they feel comfortable. It may take us longer to find full releases and uncover the person hidden beneath, but we get there. The horses support them all along this journey. Strongly logical thinking — and sometimes the medications given to my mental-health clients — can be blocks to touching what is stored deeply in the emotional body. We take a more circuitous route to reach self-awareness and self-compassion — at their pace.

They all amaze me with that part of themselves that raises the alarm when they are on a slippery slope, contemplating ending it all. Those who have stood at this precipice have a part inside that says, "Hell no, we won't go!" I assist them in finding that part and other parts of themselves to bring self-awareness. That helps them break the patterns that keep them in that dark place. They have the choice to stay or go. Many of them were never aware that it *was* a choice. This has helped a few of my clients call for help sooner rather than later. I often see patterns of negativity. We work hard on finding positivity in those times of sadness, fear, and negative thoughts. *How else can you think of this problem?*

One of my first clients was a wonderful young woman who had been battling mental-health problems since her early twenties. We will call her E. for the sake of this story.

She was doing well and really enjoyed the Gestalt method of working through her problems. We had been working together for about six months when she arrived at the arena so angry you could almost see waves of heat coming from her. With a little prompting, it blasted out of her that she was enraged at her boyfriend's wife. No judgments from me. We dove into a piece of work where she would be allowed to say whatever she needed to say to this person, with no filters. I asked if she could imagine the person in the chair, and she replied that it "wasn't ugly enough."

So, I sent her around the arena to find something to represent the "ugliness." She came back with a dirty, crumpled gray tarp and threw it in the chair. I had two horses loose in the arena with us — Gandalf the Gray and his mate, Madison. I sat slightly back but between the client and the ugly chair. Gandalf stood between the ugly chair and me, and Madison stood next to the client. Neither horse had ever been around someone angry since I had owned them. I wasn't sure what they would do, but they had sixty feet of arena to move away if they felt they needed more space.

E. launched into a furious diatribe against the woman of her focus. She screamed and swore and stomped her feet. She rose off her chair as though she was going to throw herself at the tarp and tear it to bits. Through all this harsh, extreme emotion, the two horses stood rock solid, their eyes locked on the client's eyes. This went on for about fifteen minutes. As the energy came down, E. gave the tarp a look of disdain and said, "And you can fall off the edge of the world for all I care!"

Gandalf reached over, grabbed the tarp in his teeth, and tossed it into the center of the triangle of chairs. E's eyes widened and she said to Gandalf, "You can stomp on her too!" So he did. She looked stunned and said, "You can do it more than that!" and he stomped on it three more times. E. burst into tears and cried for several minutes. While this drama played out, I had goosebumps up and down my arms. I was in awe of this horse following what she was saying. When she finished her tears, I asked what had brought them on. She said she had been a horsewoman all her life and yet had never known how much they — the horses — really understood.

Gandalf is truly a unicorn — my word for the rare horse whose intuition, steadiness, and emotional clarity make them extraordinary partners in this work. He has shown many times since just how connected he is to the client in front of him. He's kind and gently persistent until they get his message, and he can fully clear chakras. He's around thirty now, and we don't know how much longer we will have with this gem. He will always be remembered for his amazing work with people.

ON BECOMING A MASTER EQUINE GESTALTIST

At graduation in September of 2021, I signed up for the EGCM master certification program to start in 2023. That would give me another year of practice before joining another two-year program. The universe had different plans and sent me into the program a year ahead of schedule, in January of 2022. It was perfect.

My cohorts were mostly friends I had made in the EGCM program, and those who were new to me quickly became fast friends. We were together for online classes and CAMPs (in-person sessions every six months) for two years. The program delves into coaching with Gestalt methods — finding deeper meaning and more experiential ways to seek resolutions. We finished our time together with more tools to aid us in our work, more of our own personal work cleared, and a closer bond and commitment to each other. I finished with a deeper understanding of the grace and beauty of Gestalt work, no matter how hard it was at the time. I know I can call on any of these light workers and they will help me with whatever I'm facing. And I would do the same for them.

I graduated from the program with the discovery of my higher self — the person I was meant to be and could never find before. My feeling of being grounded, present, and living in a calm sense of self-confidence has also been a factor in how much trust I can gain from my clients when they meet with me. It feels good to be me now.

WHERE DOES MY NICHE LIE?

As a student in the EGCM program, I was encouraged to find a niche and go for it. I find that with my personality, variety is the spice of life. I need to be more flexible in what I do than focusing on only one niche. The ages of my clients have ranged from ten years old to the mid-sixties so far.

When I began, I was already running my own program called Energy Connected Therapeutic Horsemanship for children and teens with special needs incorporating twenty-five years of child growth and development experience and fifty-seven years of horsemanship teaching. Applying Gestalt philosophies to that program has brought more growth for the kids than my previous work. I'm more aware, grounded, and sensitive to their ability to regulate and understand.

Then mental-health patients came to That Zen Farm. I wasn't expecting to work in this specific field, yet I loved it. They fit my model of going slow and steady toward a goal of self-awareness, self-compassion, and self-discovery. I may not be able to do as much deep work as some, yet assisting them in finding light and a clear path to follow is fulfilling for them and for me.

WORKING WITH WOMEN

> "The greatest act of courage is to be and own all that you are. Without apology, without excuses, and without any masks to cover the truth of who you truly are."
>
> ~ Debbie Ford

I genuinely enjoy working with women. I love watching them find who they truly are and take the steps they design for themselves as they move toward authenticity. Some have been working in careers they thought were right for them when they were twenty, and then through life experiences — and perhaps hard times — they find themselves adrift and feeling unfulfilled. Some may even have an adult diagnosis of attention deficit disorder (sometimes with hyperactivity added), and some may have an autism diagnosis. That's a lot to carry while managing careers, children, and the ongoing demands of life.

There is a special place in my heart for working with moms of special-needs children. They have spent their child's entire life being the amplified guardian. They fight to make sure their precious child doesn't fall through the cracks of the system and receives the necessary services they need. These moms also deserve to have a full life. Somewhere along the line, they often lose who they are and what their vision of life was before the birth of their child. Through our program, they become aware of what they can accomplish when they feel whole, capable, and resourceful. The result is amazing.

I often have clients who come only one time. I don't always know that it's a one-time deal, and when that happens, I hope I hit the nail on the head and assist them in dispelling the trauma that has plagued them.

I always check in the next day to make sure they aren't walking around triggered into a place of reaction instead of response. One woman wrote:

> Yesterday was what I've been in search of for decades. There are no words to thank you for using the 'Jaws of Life' to the depth of my soul. The amount of anxiety taken away left me feeling numb, a hollow sensation in my chest today. A clear mind is a newfound freedom. The anger towards my family has been lifted while seeing them in a different light. The shackles of expectations are taken off.
>
> Do you remember me looking at you by the cube? You stood there looking back at me with no facial expression. No movement. Your eyes said everything I needed to hear.

You knew the depth of what that exercise would do for me. With your severely needed prompting, which gave me permission to express the anger I had bottled up, it was as if I was pouring out the negative feelings from the bottle to make room for the self-love. It was cleansing indeed.

The long road ahead to undo fifty-two years of stinking thinking is embraced with a knowledge base that you provided me after turning the page to my past. Thank you for taking my elementary questions seriously because that was as important as everything else. Talking to my mom behind the newspaper, tearing up that newspaper, talking to my young self (though I struggled with that), hitting the cube, going around the arena talking positively to myself, and going backwards when I spoke negatively is exactly what I needed.

Talking about my childhood had become mechanical until last night. You had me physically live every single feeling I've stuffed down for years, with it seeping out to sabotage any good relationship.

The ongoing nudging from the horse was a warm hug I could feel well into my soul. He made me feel like I wasn't alone — encouraging me to be real and honest because they were so big that nothing I could say or do could hurt him. The whole experience was by the grace of God.

Andrea, another client, wrote to me about her experience.

When I stepped into That Zen Farm in Brooklyn, Wisconsin, it was evident that this was no ordinary healing space. I met Marcy, a gifted Gestaltist (a German word for wholeness), a life coach with an incredible team of magical horses. I began working with her and learned a different approach toward finding balance and healing at a soul level in the fall of 2022. The strides I've made in my professional and personal development have been miraculous.

Marcy's approach to guidance is one-of-a-kind. Her gentle, approachable demeanor and affectionate, motherly encouragement have been pivotal in my healing process. Marcy is, without a doubt, the best at what she does. Her horses mirror her warmth, offering gentle, playful, and loving interactions that contribute significantly to the healing experience.

Participating in Marcy's weekly women's groups has been instrumental in my journey. These sessions have not only provided a supportive community but have also been a cornerstone of my success. Since beginning my work with Marcy, I have taken complete control over my life, transforming into the most authentic version of myself.

Inspired by the strength I've gained from her encouragement, I've achieved milestones I once thought were beyond my reach. I've written and published two books and now work for myself and own On Purpose Dream Consulting.

That Zen Farm, under Marcy's stewardship, is a haven for anyone seeking to embark on a journey of self-discovery and healing. For those navigating the challenges of neurodivergence and seeking holistic approaches to balance and healing, Marcy and her magical horses offer a transformative experience that is truly unmatched.

> My journey with Marcy has been a testament to the profound impact of alternative healing and compassionate support on an individual's life. I am eternally grateful to Marcy and her equine partners for guiding me through this life-changing experience!

The women who come here are often still hearing the limiting beliefs of childhood — that they "can't" or "shouldn't"—ideas from parents, grandparents, and even older siblings. The client limits themselves and their vision of who they are based on the ideas and beliefs of often well-meaning adults around them. During our sessions, we crack open those beliefs that are not their own and help them find their true values and vision.

WORKING WITH MEN

> "You must know for yourself, directly, the truth of yourself and you cannot realize it through another, however great. There is no authority that can reveal it."
>
> ~ J. Krishnamurti

Working with men has been interesting for me. My past held me back from having much to do with men. It took a while to become comfortable and to find the best way to help *them* become comfortable too. Some of my clients have had very troubling pasts — even violent at times. Many were diagnosed with autism as adults, or were not assisted when they were diagnosed as children. Our journey, with or without the horses, is about learning social patterns that are acceptable, finding focus, and exploring interests that will keep them employed or at least engaged. It is always about being aware and compassionate with themselves.

I find that the most helpful thing I can do is listen deeply. The more I listen and respond, the more they focus and stay grounded in the moment. We work on keeping conversations focused and not wandering down a different path unexpectedly. There is so much going on in their heads that it is hard to stay focused and ignore the enticing side paths that pop into mind. I have discovered that many of them have no one in their lives who can sit and listen to all the things they have been holding inside. What a release a good listener can provide.

In my experience, the school systems have improved over the years and are more successful in assisting children with ASD. There is still so much more to learn and apply. When you meet one person with autism, you've met *one* person with autism. Each presents their own unique view of the world and their own response to it.

Most of my adult clients have been through the mental-health system and received their diagnosis while being evaluated during a crisis in their lives. The older the client, the less they received from their school — though this varies from district to district, and often depends on the size of the school and its budget. When they didn't receive services, they seem to have more mental-health issues, more anger, and more difficulty with social interactions and understanding social rules. I see low self-esteem, shut-down self-awareness, and very little self-compassion. The negativity of life fires up first, and it takes effort to find the light in any situation.

One of the men wrote the following note to me:

> This program helped me gain more confidence in myself. But it also gave me a calm. Being on the farm, being with the horses and having them work around and on me helped work out my issues. It helped me a lot. Gandalf helped me come out of my shell. When we do the 'I Thou' meditation it is very peaceful. And when I went to

martial arts competitions, I felt more like the martial artist I'm striving to be. I had a centered focus and a strong concentration that couldn't be broken. I won my class because I felt in harmony.

Marcy and her horses help chase my problems away. And they were like builders, helping me build blocks of myself up to be something greater. You helped me get to where I wanted to be in life. I had to answer two big questions: "Who was I?" and "What did I want from life?"

WORKING WITH YOUTH AND TEENS

"There is hope and strength in understanding."

~ Dr. Temple Grandin

Working with youth and teens is somewhat different from working with adults. They are not fully developed yet and are still figuring out who they are — and that changes quickly. We explore how to respond instead of react to problems. We imagine who they think or feel they will be when they are grown. We make vision boards. We explore fear and courage, and release anger when we can. I have several youths in the county mental-health program who have mental-health issues as well as autism, ADHD, depression, and other blocks to discovering who they are.

In my younger clients, I see more hope as school districts and counties find more therapies for their young people. There is more awareness in the community to support the child and the whole family. There are more ways for the child to understand, communicate, and make sense of what they are going through. It gives me hope.

WOMEN'S CIRCLE GROUPS

"The circle of women around us weave invisible nets
of love that carry us when we are weak and
sing with us when we are strong."

~ Sark

I love working privately, and I love working with groups. Group work is a whole different dynamic than private clients. It's amazing to see what happens when you put a group of strangers together and assist them in weaving a bond so strong that they can support each other even when they are no longer here. I experienced this myself during my two years becoming a Master Gestaltist. We had the same group of women who met weekly for class on Zoom and met twice a year in Colorado for deep Gestalt training. We became bonded in a way I had never experienced before. The feelings for each other go deeper than socio-economic levels, educational background, religion, or political ideology. We found common ground to stand on. It began with horses and Gestalt and turned into more than friendship. I know I can call on any one of them at any time when I need them. We have each other's backs.

THE BEAUTY OF GROUPS

The beauty of groups is that they allow us to run more experiments, find loving support, and receive the borrowed benefits that come from helping one another through experiential work. In this shared space, trust is allowed to seep into the soul. I often hear at the end of a piece of emotional work, "I thought I was alone! I never knew anyone else experienced this. I learned so much about myself during your piece of work!"

The beauty of Gestalt lies in its ability to create a space in which we become deeply — physically and emotionally — involved in discovering both the source and healing of our trauma. I listen closely to what is said, and all members of the group can become parts in the drama, reenactment, or incident. By stepping in and out of the creation, the client is able to uncover the answers they have been seeking and to resolve past trauma. It's a time to give in and freely experience the emotions and say the words the client couldn't say at the time of the trauma. Some clients have had mothers who didn't know how to mother, fathers who hurt them, or a death in the family of a beloved sibling or grandparent. The gamut of what we put ourselves through when we feel guilty — or *are* guilty — is wide and deep. Having a group of loving, supportive people to hold you during this vulnerable emotional time is the grace of group work. The women often continue their friendship after leaving the group as soul sisters.

Fostering trust in each other — and in me — is paramount to honest emotional release. I establish, reiterate, and continually reinforce an atmosphere of safety and security: a sacred place where participants are free to be themselves. The horses and I are calm, confident, compassionate, and in the moment for everyone, at all times.

I was terrified to start a group at first. Now I miss it when we don't have one going. Winters in Wisconsin — even with a warm, cozy lounge — can be too cold, snowy, and windy to make the drive to the farm appealing. Januarys are especially quiet around here, and that is when I recharge and renew my reserves.

After the initial fear that I would forget all my training, I fell into the flow of the group's energy. I listened deeply, asked the right questions at the right time, and created experiential exercises that allowed participants to work through whatever had come into their awareness. I discovered that I loved the work. Together, we delved deeply into who they were innately and what barriers stood between them and that authentic self.

At the end of each week's session, I ask what they are leaving with after their time together. Their answers often touch each other's hearts. They often ask me what *I* am leaving with as well. I always thank them for teaching me more about who they are and how I can assist them. I tell them how grateful I am that they trusted me to keep them safe in a secure and sacred place to do their work and heal. My heart is filled with compassion and love for them and their journeys.

Seeing them grow and heal also allows me to do the same. My values of compassion and making a difference are deeply involved in this work. I love watching them grow and fly from the nest. My work fills me up and reenergizes me.

RACHEL'S STORY

To close this chapter, allow me to share the remarkable story of Rachel, one of my group students:

> My son was already a part of That Zen Farm's Energy Connected Therapeutic Horsemanship program. When Marcy offered a Moms Equine Gestalt Group, I jumped at the chance to join. The group was mostly made up of moms of children with special needs.
>
> As I arrived that first night, I felt a sense of peace and safety. I had support from other women. I'd been isolated and taught to be completely dependent upon my husband. I lived in fear and treaded very lightly around the house, unsure of when the next blowup would be. I kept the peace because that was safer for me. I was completely unmotivated to do anything outside of caring for my children. My mental health was so bad I was almost incompetent. I could never have figured this all out on my own. Somehow, this felt like Divine intervention.

I have always loved horses, and I owned a horse when I was a teenager. One of the horses in the arena waiting for us was a beautiful gray named Gandalf. He came to me as I sat in the 'People Pen.' He placed his lips and muzzle on my shoulder and the side of my neck. Occasionally, he would try to tip my ballcap off my head. I would cram it back down hard each time. The energy I felt from him was very intense, and yet he stood absolutely still. I had no fear of him even though he was right in my face. It was amazing and peaceful. I had never experienced anything like it. There was something very different about him. I felt it was important to allow him to do whatever he was doing. When he finally moved away, I realized that the pain I had for several months in my neck was gone. On my way home, I realized just how healing horses can be.

The next time we gathered, I did a big piece of work on my feelings of worthlessness. I had been broken down for years by domestic abuse from the one person I thought loved me. His narcissistic tendencies and manipulations had me feeling unworthy, stupid, and defeated. I had no energy to fight. I didn't even try to tell anyone what was going on — no one ever believed me.

We did a piece called 'Belief Cones.' Midway through, I felt the horses supporting me. I could feel the empathy and support of the women in the circle as I shared my goal of finding my worth and the actions I would take to get there. I was finally heard. I found the confidence to get it all out in the open. It was really hard to do. Saying it all out loud and walking the ball diamond of cones eased the way. I realized that the change started with me. *I* was the starting point. I needed to find the courage and confidence to make the change. One of the results would be that my children would get to see me happy instead of afraid. At the end, I cried and cried in the arms of the women. I also gained confidence while listening to their stories of trauma.

Every week I learned something new about myself. I had buried so much. I learned about the values I live by. I found self-awareness. I learned about the parts of myself that were true but buried beneath parts that had kept me safe. My sense of worth and confidence were two of those I needed to call forward to help me on my journey. I learned I can do whatever I need to do to reach my goal. I became aware of how my upbringing set me up for the life through which I was currently suffering. I had already changed that pattern for my children. Even as a young mom, I knew I would do anything to stop that generational trauma. They are loved, nurtured, and strong.

One day my husband threatened me with a gun. I thought I was going to die. Our group met that day, and I talked about what happened. Marcy set up a physical boundary and asked me what he had to do to me or the children before I acted. She kept shoving that boundary at me and asking, 'How about now?' Where was the line he had to cross? I had never set boundaries. I didn't know how. I felt that if I set boundaries, I would be setting myself up for more violence from him. So I did nothing.

During the piece of work, I realized that nothing was stopping him from hurting his children. I was shocked by that awareness. I knew then that he had already crossed the line, and I had to act. I went home and started divorce proceedings. I found the confidence, my self-worth, and the ability to speak the truth in court. I won a ten-year restraining order to protect us all. Each time I had to appear in court to fight another battle with him, I brought Gandalf's energy with me and wore my cowgirl boots to remind me of my strength.

I found my self-compassion. I had never had that before. I always worried and fretted over every mistake I made or was told I had made. I would try to figure out what I had done wrong, what I could have changed, what I *should* have done. Now that I am living my true values and being self-compassionate, that pattern of self-recrimination has stopped.

I had been spiritually disconnected and had looked long and hard to find my connection to spirit. Doing the Gestalt work around what caused the blocks made all the difference. It felt like Divine intervention once I started opening up. Gandalf was a huge part of that discovery. He is a gift to the world.

We spent time finding our vision for ourselves and creating a vision board. I keep mine in my bedroom where I can see it every day. My circumstances have changed since creating it, but the vision remains clear, and I work toward it every day. I was trained to believe that I needed my husband to do anything in this world. I didn't. It's been a wild journey this past year, and my story isn't finished yet. I am fearless, I am confident, and I trust myself to make the right decisions for my family and myself. I'm in the process of finding the career path that best suits me. I have truly figured out who I am. And best of all, my home is a place of peace.

CHAPTER FIVE

OUR PROGRAM AND OUR BUSINESS

"Well, now that we have met each other," said the unicorn, "if you'll believe in me, I will believe in you."

~ Lewis Carroll

I would love to see multiple groups — women, teens, parents, and men — come to That Zen Farm every week. My vision is to grow the farm into a place where other Equine Gestalt coaches can practice and where the Energy Connected Therapeutic Horsemanship program can also flourish. There is room for growth and time for financial planning to be done. I feel that the next ten years will be spent working to fulfill my vision of educating horsemanship teachers and creating sacred space for Equine Gestalt to happen. By the time I hit my eightieth year, I'm sure I'll feel the need to slow down.

In 2024, two of our older lesson ponies became ill with unknown illnesses. We searched for answers, but it was a fruitless effort. We were only able to treat the symptoms without knowing the cause. We did our best to maintain their health. I make a lifelong commitment to my equine partners no matter what happens to them or how old they live to be. They let me know when they are ready to pass over the rainbow bridge. Billy Bob made a full recovery. Sadly, we lost

Naughty John in early 2025. My herd of well-trained unicorns was shrinking. I began the hunt for replacements for my aging herd.

SEEKING THE UNICORN

For me, a unicorn needs many special qualities. They also need specialized training and a tolerance for things far outside the normal horse-and-rider realm. I have trained all the horses we partner with now, but my business is fast and furious, and I have little time to train horses anymore. Finding a new unicorn who does not require extensive additional training for this work is challenging, and the cost of well-trained horses is beyond our current budget. Thankfully, I have two people who help get new horses ready: Lily Zunker, who grew up in the program and now helps me teach young riders, and Heather McManamy who does positive reinforcement training. Even for me, there is still a lot to learn. I'm very interested in this mode of training and squeeze in a lesson a week when I can.

The unicorn I'm looking for will be calm, with more whoa than go. They will meet new situations with curiosity rather than fear. I look for kindness and a desire to be with people. I look for a willingness to make a connection, both on the ground and with a rider in the saddle. I also look for that care for the rider that comes from all the virtues above. They will stop if the rider is off balance or isn't making a clear intention.

A lot of current training methods rely on pressure and discipline that no longer suit my training style or the needs of special kids. I have found that when fear tactics or overly desensitized horses finally have a chance to say no, they say it in a big way.

Many of the youth who come here have never been close to a large animal. Even a pony can seem huge to them. Most of my ponies are between 800 and 900 pounds and are taller than the children who ride them. Some of these children don't understand that quick, unregulated movements and loud noises can trigger a horse to flee. The emotional roller coaster of happy loud laughter, screaming cries, or an occasional raging meltdown can cause a horse to think "DANGER!" Unicorns need to be that mystical beast who can take it all in and let it out again without needing to escape. Deep inside, they want to heal whatever wounds affect their little partner. They want to be there.

The mystical beast needs excellent ground manners. They need to be easily haltered, led gracefully, and able to stand for grooming and tacking up with peace and patience. They need to follow unclear body language and figure out where the person wants them to go, even when the focus is sketchy at best. We teach everyone how to groom and saddle when they are ready. For some, it looks like three or four swipes with a brush; for others, it's full grooming with love. I use a timer with some and encouragement with all. And I make sure the horse is groomed by the volunteer if the student can't or won't because of sensory issues, strength issues, or excitement to be on the horse.

The unicorn must see the mounting block as a great place to be. They need to stand quietly for mounting, girth tightening, stirrup adjustments, and instructions to the rider, and then wait for the cue to move forward. My horses work with the client through the use of energy focused on the desired direction. When that concept isn't understood by the rider, and if they are able to speak, we ask them to use vocal commands. If that isn't possible, the volunteer horse leader gives the verbal cue to get the horse started.

The unicorn must walk with a steady, even footfall. When being ridden, the unicorn must be aware of the rider's balance. If the rider slips to one side or leans too far forward or back, the horse should stop and let the helpers know something is amiss. The unicorn needs to be a slow, deep breather; this comes naturally to a calm and confident horse. This regulates the rider's breathing as well. The horse regulating itself assists the rider in regulating themselves.

We mostly walk, with maybe a little trotting. I currently have no horses who can canter consistently with a rider, and I'm very careful with my riders. I don't want an injured rider or an insurance claim looming over my head. If I could find a unicorn who could walk, trot, canter, and jump low jumps — and didn't break the bank — I'd seriously consider it.

When we must, we create our unicorns. I recently adopted two mares we fostered from Spirit Horse Rescue and Education Center in Janesville, Wisconsin. We have spent the last two years teaching them our gentler way of working with horses. They are progressing and are catching on to the fact that we respect a no and rejoice when we get a yes.

Raya, one of the mares, was reluctant to be ridden without someone leading her. She seemed confused when no one was walking beside her. She never said no to anything except walking off alone. Heather, our positive reinforcement trainer, found a game to help her find her independence and confidence.

Izzy, the other mare, did everything you asked — but out of fear. She would freeze if you pushed through her very quiet no. She was afraid to make a mistake, likely from past punishment. Instead of working through a scary situation, Izzy would stop her feet and her mind. I could tell when she was reaching her tipping point: her nose would wrinkle, her nostrils widen, and her eyes go wide. At that point she would either freeze or begin to wiggle around. When she reached the fidget-and-fuss stage, grooming and saddling became difficult. She built on that energy until she couldn't stand at the mounting block. When we first started working with her, we purposely ignored her no to see what she would do. She said no louder and had to be asked several times to stand at the mounting block. Interestingly, once a rider was in the saddle, she acted quiet — but she would freeze up.

We began working through each step slowly until she relaxed. Lots of praise and breaks in between. It has taken her two years to come up to me in the pasture for petting and scratching. For me, that's a huge leap forward from avoiding me and making me follow her around to halter her. Recently, we switched to Positive Reinforcement training. She is literally eating it up and has made giant strides toward trust, problem-solving, and confidence.

I have made a commitment of care and growth to both mares. I can see the great horses within them and will wait until they are ready to be great teachers in the school.

I loved the Gypsy horses I met at Touched By A Horse in Colorado. They are gentle and remarkably attuned to people. In the spring of 2024, I purchased a Gypsy/Quarter Horse yearling, Lil' Lizzie. She has another four years of learning ahead of her before she can work in the program, yet she is already showing signs of being a unicorn. She follows children around, stands quietly without a halter for grooming, and even walks to the mounting block so a child can reach her back. We recently added Gabriel, a yearling full Gypsy Vanner gelding, to our herd. He is a total sweetheart with a tremendous potential to become a unicorn as well.

As the horse and rider walk, remarkable changes are taking place in the rider's brain. Jen Bluske, an amazing children's occupational therapist, shared that research shows new neural pathways are created by the movement of the horse. We can see this in the rider's whole body and facial expressions. They start off stiff, bracing, or unable to sit upright. Their face might appear happy, yet apprehensive. As the horse continues to move, the rider begins to flow with the motion, breathe more slowly, and release tension from their face. Many parents say this is the only place they see their child smile.

The more work the horse does on the child, the quicker the child tires. There is so much input coming to the rider that it can be almost overwhelming. I watch closely for that overstimulation line. I try to find the fine line between enough and too much. I want to end on a note of fulfillment and satisfaction — not overload.

The size of the unicorn matters. For younger riders, I like a unicorn to be 12.2 to 14 hands (50–56 inches at the withers) with good bone and body size. I have had many Haflingers over the past 26 years, and they have been great for clients up to about 150 pounds. For riders over five feet tall or with more weight, I choose a taller horse. I have a Clydesdale for riders over 200 pounds. I also consider the needs of the volunteer who walks next to the rider. I try to match the volunteer to the horse and rider whenever possible. If they have to support the rider's leg, they need to be comfortable for the duration of the lesson. Sadly, volunteers are often the last to get what they need, as I am more focused on the match between horse and rider — emotionally and physically.

The unicorn needs to be emotionally mature and confident enough to handle the emotional journey of their human partners. Even as they love people and willingly step forward to do the work, they feel the emotional energy of those they support. Although horses are adept at releasing tension and adrenaline, they can still become drained after a while. They need to be taken out of the lineup before they reach the end of their emotional bank. We must watch for changes in the horse's behavior, however subtle. Listening for that no saves them from a possible breakdown. A wrinkled nostril can turn into a bite. A jiggle during saddling can turn into a bigger issue. A tail swish can lead to a kick — maybe not today, but someday. Why not listen? Why not give them downtime and a chance to regroup?

Summers are full of long days and back-to-back clients. That's when we make our biggest income. Horses are not cheap to care for, especially when you are also dedicated to caring for the elderly who can no longer work. It's not an easy decision to pull a horse from the lineup when there is pressure to fulfill the promise of riding to clients. I plan for each of my horses to take a full year off whenever I can. This gives them more years to be part of the work and gives them a break from the emotional energy and demand. It's harder when I am down a couple of horses at the start of the season. I now take the whole month of January off to make sure everyone gets rest — me included. I couldn't do this when I first started, but now my income is enough to cover the lack of clients for a month.

The price for unicorns is high — often over $10,000 for a horse that may not even meet my guidelines. Most sellers require full payment upfront rather than offering a payment plan. I have saved for the last few years to afford suitable replacements. The most important virtue is the horse's personality. I like to visit and assess prospects. This past year, when I bought the young Gypsies, I had to rely on the breeder's assessment of their personalities. So far, they have been right on. Sadly, there are unscrupulous dealers out there. It's wise to have a prepurchase exam and find a reputable hauler. I have added insurance on the more expensive horses. All of this adds to the total cost of finding replacements.

When I pay over $3,000 for a horse, I insure it. To me, that's a lot of money down the drain if the horse dies unexpectedly. The policies I have also cover a certain amount for colic care.

What if I buy a horse that ultimately doesn't fit the program? It's certainly possible, especially if I can't meet the horse in person. With my years of experience training horses, I could likely bring such a horse along, but I am very careful in what I buy. I have been extremely fortunate when I purchased what my heart told me to do.

CREATING A BEAUTIFUL, WONDERFUL WORKSPACE

It's not all about the horses. It's about the *feel* of the place. I started small — so small. I had a 45' by 45' area inside the barn and an outdoor riding arena. Gradually, over the years, we were able to add an indoor arena with funds that my husband's mother left us. She supported special-needs groups for years, and Dale felt it was an appropriate way to honor her.

We added fruit trees along the drive. We — and I really mean my husband, Dale — keep the area around the barns clean, mowed, weed-free, and inviting. I made a rock garden and flower beds in front of the arena to draw people in.

A few years ago, I cashed in my retirement fund and built a heated/air-conditioned lounge for everyone to use when needed. That has been well-received with Wisconsin's cranky weather changes. I created within its walls a place of peace and safety to allow sharing those hard emotions more easily. It's filled with cheery colors and comfy chairs, a fireplace, and refreshments — a homey feel. I didn't mean to add therapy cats, but they came anyway. All but one just showed up and became part of the ambience. The best one was my grandchildren's cat, who came here after they sold their farm. Tigey thinks it's his job to soothe anyone who sits in the chairs in the arena or lounge.

I work seven days a week. Last year, I scheduled a day off each week. This year, I have too many clients for that luxury. I love my work, and it gives me the energy to keep going. And when clients cancel, I take the time off to rest. There is always winter to rest when the clients decide to stay warm at home.

For the last two years, I have had an assistant (she's now a teacher here) to help me teach, and several volunteers to help in the arena. I have boarders who help with chores and putting hay up during haymaking season. I imagine I will be adding more helpers as I age.

BEST BUSINESS PRACTICES

It's a great idea to learn how to run a business before you actually run a business. I ran a few businesses before this one. They weren't failures, but they also didn't thrive. I needed to learn more and understand more before I could truly make a profit. The most important aspect for me was understanding that I was **worthy of abundance**. Abundance is not only about money, but also about accepting love, learning, friendship, and whatever else creates a feeling of wholeness. Then I needed a clear vision of what I wanted this business to look like. I had to figure out my values, my niche, and my goals — and then make a clear plan to get where I wanted to go.

I hired a great accountant and tax professional, as soon as I could afford them, to advise me and keep me on top of the government tax requirements.

I also continue to learn and grow in my specific areas of expertise. I read, watch, and engage in continuing-education opportunities. I will never know it all, but I can strive for that.

Insurance

We live in a litigious society. I have carried insurance for all the years I have taught lessons, and I purchased special insurance for the Equine Gestalt work. The substantial amount I pay is worth its weight in gold if something happens here on the farm. Horses are wonderful, and yet they can make mistakes that can injure. We also have safety rules around the horses, farm equipment, haystacks, and pasture entry. Parental supervision is imperative. I also work slowly and safely. I know my horses very well before they are asked to work with either program.

Horses for the Job

I've already discussed what a unicorn for the riding program looks like. And any horse who wants to do Gestalt work can do so. Some may not be interested, some are hesitant, some lack trust, and some jump right in. Some are picky about who they work with, and some embrace — literally wrapping their heads and necks around a person — everyone they encounter. I have several different breeds and a mix of mares and geldings. They range in age from their teens to thirty years old. I don't use horses under the age of five for this emotional work. I allow them to mature without that pressure. I start them slowly, only a couple of clients per week in the beginning. The emotional health of my herd is an important part of their care. I don't want them to burn out or cross the boundary of good manners.

It's interesting to observe who shows up when we are in session. I usually have two horses who are pastured together in the arena at a time. The horses are sensing where the person is emotionally as soon as they enter the arena. Horses feel this emotional vibration, and it's my job to help the client get out of their head and into their feelings. The horses do their best work when the person is present and in the moment.

My Current Horse Partners

Gandalf the Gray

Gandalf is the top unicorn of my herd. He looks mostly Quarter Horse, although we don't know for sure. He can show up for clients in many ways. He was balancing my chakras before I even knew what that was — I only knew I felt better when he walked away. He's the only horse here who can lower physical pain as well as emotional pain.

I used to get frequent headaches, and one of my boarders had stomach pains. Gandalf would approach me when I was sitting on the mounting block and gently put his head on mine, never pushing or using his lips. He would stay in that position for over a minute, and when he moved away, the headache would be gone.

Gandalf was instrumental in soothing pain for one of my boarders as well. He placed the length of his head against her chest and abdomen, breathed on her with deep breaths, and when he walked away minutes later, her pain was gone. He has cleared ailments for other people too.

He also balances chakras. He can find the chakra area where the client is having trouble and use his nose to pinpoint the spot, often staying a minute or two. When asked what they think he's doing, the client often launches into a story about what is bothering them — and it often lines up with the chakra he's touching.

His most amazing talent is understanding what is going on during an experiential experience. He often joins in and assists clients in seeing what they may not have been able to see before. He's thirty-one years old at this writing. Every morning I hope to find him still with us and ready for breakfast.

Madison

Madison is Gandalf's longtime girlfriend. She is a beautiful dark liver-chestnut Morgan horse. She was quite hesitant to start doing Gestalt work. At first, she would stay on the far side of the arena and watch. As she observed and learned from Gandalf, she became more familiar with the process and moved closer to the clients. Eventually she found her place holding space for people who were working on themselves. She has expanded to help others find their boundaries. Recently she has been active in the experiments and is understanding more about her job.

A MADISON STORY: A client arrived a bit late, and Madison met her at the gate. She stayed with the woman, even when the woman came inside the People Pen. The People Pen keeps the horses loose and free on the outside and allows the clients to sit without the horse getting in the middle of the circle.

Once I found the door to open the piece of work for the woman, we set up an experiment outside the pen. Madison stayed with the woman but didn't interfere. The experiment ended, and the woman was relieved of her burden. We were walking back to the pen when Madison suddenly moved rapidly in our direction. She approached the woman from the rear, very carefully stepped on the side of the woman's shoe, and hip-checked her, knocking her to the sand.

I was shocked — I had never seen her do that before. I gently removed her hoof from the woman's shoe and helped the client up. I softly admonished Madison, reminding her to use gentler measures in the future. I turned to the client and asked what she thought it meant.

To my surprise, she laughed. She said that all week she had been saying to nurses and doctors, "I don't mean to step on toes but…" I asked about the second part of Madison's message. She said, "When life knocks you down, you get up and meet it again!"

The Rose

The Rose, a beautiful gray Arabian mare, came to us from a sheriff's department animal-neglect seizure. She was starved, neglected, and treated very roughly. She had two foals. The younger one, a two-year-old filly, survived only because Rose continued to nurse her when most mares would have weaned her before six months old. Rose's body condition was so low the veterinarians didn't think she would make it. Through a carefully planned, enriching diet and lots of love, we nursed her through her depression and trauma.

Rose loves holding space with the moms of children with special needs.

One day a mother and son arrived for the son's therapeutic riding lesson. I noticed the mom was upset and teary-eyed. She came into the arena and sat on the mounting block after her son mounted his horse. The Rose approached her ever so slowly. The woman had no prior experience with horses and was a bit afraid of them. A change was about to occur.

Rose eased up to the block and placed herself in front of the woman. She gently lowered her muzzle into the mom's lap. The woman's eyes widened, and ever so carefully she began stroking Rose's face. They stayed that way for most of the hour-long lesson.

When I asked what had made her so sad, she said she hadn't slept well the night before, worrying about her son's future. He's on the autism spectrum, and their days were filled with therapists, school, medications, doctors, and support for them all. She said it was overwhelming. She commented that Rose made her feel calm — and that she felt everything would be okay.

Rose often gravitates toward moms and young children. She has stepped in to help me many times, even though she had been so badly treated in her previous home. She is now thirty years old. We love this beautiful girl and will care for her until it's her time.

Naughty John

During the writing of this book, Naughty John passed over the rainbow bridge.

When I met John for the first time, he was a yearling and as cute as a button. He tucked his head under my arm and followed me on the tour of the owner's horses. He never left my side. I told the man that this one was going home with me.

I brought him and his half-brother home and watched them grow. John became quite an escape artist. He could crawl through a four-strand electric fence and not disturb a thing. He was super easy to train and never took a wrong step. His heart was pure gold.

When I would tell people his full name, they would laugh. I would whisper that we don't tell him the "Naughty" part. He was three-quarters Haflinger and one-quarter Quarter Horse — a great combination. He was about 13.2 hands, perfect for kids yet big enough for a small adult.

He was our laugh-a-day guy. He did well no matter who rode him — but only when the rider asked him correctly. His curiosity sometimes got him into trouble. He picked things up and carried them around, knocked over obstacles, pushed the ball around the arena, and rolled the barrels. He was a constant reminder that there needs to be fun in the day as well as work. He also snuggled with clients — that was his most redeeming trait.

We will miss him and his humorous antics. Run free, beautiful boy.

Nein

Nein is a registered Haflinger Horse. He's Naughty John's half-brother, born two weeks after John. He is twenty-two years old at this writing. Nein was my stallion for three years, and he has one baby who is now eighteen. He was a good stallion, and he's an even better gelding.

We started him working with kids this year, and his favorite part is connecting with them on the ground and doing whatever the child wants to do. He loves going through the obstacle course with only a connection of energy and focused destination — no lead line needed. I feel he will be great at this work with time and practice.

Maya

Maya is a bay Clydesdale with a huge heart. I purchased her for my larger clients, as most of my horses are under fifteen hands high. A hand is four inches, measured at the horse's withers. Maya is small for a Clyde at about 16.3 hands (66 inches).

She enjoys working on the ground more than riding. She is still working on relaxing when ridden. One of our young men who works with her on the ground said he likes her because she's the only girl who makes him feel normal-sized. The opposite could be true too — he makes her look "normal" size.

She helps people feel calm through her slow, easy breathing, steady heart rate, and warm body. She invites clients to draw close, supporting them in becoming grounded and peaceful. It's amazing to watch them soften and melt under her care.

CHAPTER SIX

SENSORY EXPECTATIONS

"I must remind myself that my task is to help children feel strong within themselves."

~ Violet Oaklander, *Windows to Our Children*

A farm is a place of huge sensory experiences. There could be a quiet meow from one of the barn cats, the smell of horses and manure, the flitting and chatter of sparrows, sunlight, shadows, wind. The energy of the horses can be a blessing or an overwhelm depending on the person who is receiving it. A farm can be a lot for many clients who have trouble handling themselves with sensory overload. Reactions can vary, and I must be prepared for those.

Many ASD people, both children and adults, have sensory difficulties. Sensory integration disorder (SID) is a neurological condition that occurs when the brain is unable to process sensory information. It can affect one or more senses, including hearing, vision, motor function, touch, taste, and smell. The best way to help clients with this is through self-regulation, patterns, and a healthy (horse-sized) dose of patience. This is an area where the horses excel.

I have noticed that many of my clients have sensory issues, ranging from over- or under-response, or seeking input, to extreme sensitivity to light, smells, sounds, and nearly everything else. How difficult it must be to be deluged by everything around you.

SENSORY EXPERIENCE

When I write about sensory experience, a few quotes from my clients immediately pop into my mind. Ali M. said to me one day, "I'm going to hug you, Marcy, even if you do smell like a horse." That's okay, Ali — I love you too.

I am also inspired by Naoki Higashida, a thirteen-year-old nonspeaking autistic boy from Japan, who wrote in *The Reason I Jump*, **"True compassion is not about bruising the other person's self-respect."**

I am inspired by my clients' ability to work past the fear of bugs, heat and cold, smells, and noises to be with the horse. They work hard to hold a curry comb or a brush, feel the coarseness of the mane and tail, and touch the softness of the muzzle. It may be the first time they allow their hands to get dirty — and then wait until the end of the session to wash that dirt off. Most of all, I am touched and inspired by their desire to trust the horse and allow themselves to leave the ground and let the horse take care of them.

WHAT I SEE

I often see that the same awareness that keeps horses watchful and ready to flee is also present in clients with sensory processing disorder. Some clients look at things a bit sideways, like a skeptical horse. It may be worry, or simply how they need to look at things to see them better. They may turn away from — or even gag at — the scent of horse manure. They may jump at the slightest sounds. They may not like the feel of the brush, the curry, or even the horse's mane and tail. Many don't like it when I touch them.

I especially see the loss of balance when the horse moves under them. It can be a combination of some or all of these sensitivities, mild to extreme. Some clients show very little response to stimuli — these are the ones who like the bumpy trot the most. We work to find a way to bring awareness to all the clients.

I also see the love of the horse. And I see trust grow each time they arrive. I see confidence grow. I see them taking on new responsibility and awareness of themselves and the world around them.

WHAT WE DO

We often work in the indoor arena to cut down on some of the sensory input. That helps me gauge what the client may or may not tolerate. The reaction of the individual sets how we will proceed. A client who is easily overstimulated may take weeks to be able to walk from the parking area to the arena to touch the horse. Every step is huge for them. It matters to me that they are allowed to absorb what they can in their own time. We can connect in so many ways even before we get to the horses.

Pat Parelli, founder of the Natural Horsemanship program, has often said, **"Take the time it takes so it takes less time."** I find this applies to humans as well as to horses.

One of my first special-needs clients was very sensitive to noise. I am so used to the sounds around the farm that I block out a lot of annoying noises. This child arrived one day ready to ride. As she climbed down out of her mom's van, a rooster crowed right next to the vehicle. She was so alarmed that, despite trying many weeks of headphones and other strategies, we had to give up. It was a sad day for me. The chickens are part of our farm family, so they stay on as part of the charm — and part of the noise. I've never had the problem again, and I hope I never do.

The clients who need more stimulation and input are usually up and in the saddle on the first day. They seem to sense that they will be filled up by the movement of the horse.

In deciding which horse will work best with the client, I rely on my knowledge of my horses' personalities and what I feel the child needs to build a partnership with that horse. It's important to me to find a partner who can assist them in building trust, connection, communication, and friendship.

WHERE DO WE BEGIN?

"Neurodiversity is a mosaic of minds,
each with its own brilliance."

~ Anonymous

Our clients have a wide range of neurological conditions, including ASD, developmental disorders, PTSD, anxiety, and other mental-health diagnoses. We also have a handful of typically developing children.

We take the time it takes to learn about each person who comes here. I read the goals that have been set by the agency the client works with, or from the parents and guardians. Then I put them away and get to know the person who shows up in my arena. No assumptions. No judgment. Only compassion, empathy, and an openness to begin exactly where they are in that moment. We build on what they already know and can do, with patience and care.

Horses are natural healers. I see them connecting with our clients on so many levels of care. They give feelings of safety and warmth. They use their inner energy to lift people from sadness or anger into a place that feels lighter and calmer. Their body movements create new pathways in the brain. Their slow, deep breathing eases our tight, short breaths. Their warmth seeps into the clients.

SELF-REGULATION

Our goal of self-regulation is often a difficult journey, and that is true for both neurodivergent and neurotypical people, young or old. Most of us can have bouts of dysregulation, but we don't have to live with it all the time as many of my clients do. Arlin Cuncic, MA, describes dysregulation as "an inability to control or regulate one's emotional responses, which can lead to mood swings, significant changes in mood, or emotional lability (constantly changing)."

While dysregulation is often thought of as a childhood problem that resolves as children mature, sometimes the child doesn't find resolution. That can cause lifelong challenges, including facing difficulties in school, maintaining relationships, or functioning in the workplace.

If the dysregulation is part of a diagnosed mental disorder, the person is less able to return to a "normal" state within a reasonable amount of time after being exposed to emotional stimuli. The reaction may be over the top compared to the situation that caused it. They may not be able to calm down, avoid tough emotions, or resist impulsive actions. They may not even have awareness when they are rapidly heading down that highly emotional road.

In children, dysregulation can involve tantrums, refusing to look at or speak to another person, crying, hitting, and more. They may have trouble sleeping, hang on to experiences, blow things out of proportion, struggle socially, or even engage in self-harm or harm to others.

At That Zen Farm, we see many young people with this type of emotional reaction and the consequences that follow. We work on self-awareness and recognizing when they are reacting rather than responding. We talk about how the horse can be a reactive animal and what that looks like. They observe how the horse calms itself and returns to a state of relaxation. They learn to respond to the horse's fear by being calm and breathing deeply *for* the horse. When they see that they can calm the horse, they realize they can accomplish it for themselves. I often hear parents say their child was calmer and had fewer meltdowns for the entire week after their lesson.

The horse also works to calm the client when the client is reactive. It's a beautiful two-way street. I work to be a co-regulator. I am blessed with an inner calm that has come with time, years of working with hundreds of people, and most importantly, my personal Gestalt work.

I learned early in my horse career that my emotional levels can affect the horse. I now see that the one emotion they respond to most strongly is fear. On the opposite end, they will ignore a person who is "in their head" and not present in the moment. I learned to use deep, regulated breathing and stay in the moment. It has become my norm. I model this behavior for clients and assist them in finding what works for them.

We work to keep routines the same until the client is ready for a change — one that will help them grow and improve their skills. When I notice something that is a trigger, we find a way to work around it or work through it. I am upfront, honest, and very gentle with my clients. I want them to see that I am aware of their reactions, never judgmental of them, and that my goal is to help them to be able to notice and understand those reactions for themselves.

When I become aware of a block that may lead to frustration, fear, or anger, I talk with the parents to ensure shared understanding and support. I also speak candidly to the client about what I observe. Together, we explore the emotion — what it is, where they feel it in their body, and what steps we can take to move forward without being blocked by the emotion that arises. When things go well, we celebrate enthusiastically. I tell my clients exactly what they did well and how their actions supported their goals.

Self-regulation is difficult for anyone. When adding the process of learning how to communicate with a 1,000-pound horse, you may see reaction instead of response. One of the greatest challenges for clients with regulation struggles is adjusting to a new horse and building a trusting, effective partnership.

Our goal here is to assist the client in finding self-awareness — to recognize that moment when they slip from being present into frustration, fear, anger, or overwhelm. Then to take that breath and give the whole situation a pause to see whether the reaction is needed or whether a calmer response would be more helpful.

There are times when it *is* appropriate to react. Being authentic to what the client is feeling is a true path, and acknowledging that emotion matters. What we do next is important. Can the client breathe through it? Do they need a string of swear words to clear the air? Do they need to cry and let that deep emotion out?

I have noticed that many of my clients feel deeply that everything that goes wrong is their fault. Several ask if I am mad at them or apologize repeatedly. I usually bring it back to awareness and ask if I've ever been mad at them before. When they say no, I ask what they felt they had done to bring up the apology. They may not know — and that's fine. The question is simply to bring awareness. I reassure them that I will tell them when I am angry and why. They will not have to guess. Another challenge is the belief that they must do everything perfectly. I don't ask for perfection; I ask only that they do the best they can in that moment.

We work to find self-compassion. It's not wrong to have strong reactions. I ask that they take responsibility for their actions and then find compassion for themselves. If they truly did something they feel is wrong, we talk about what action they can take next time that would be more appropriate.

It amazes me how calmly the horses deal with anger and frustration. They support clients with quiet steadfastness. I was taught as a young teacher that horses will run away from strong displays of emotion — and yet, that has not been my experience. They stay close, sometimes close enough to touch, while anger and despair pour out. If strong emotions happen in the saddle, I ask the client to get down so the horse can help from the ground. I rarely see anger once a client is on the horse; being with the horse is so calming that it rarely appears.

It can take years for a person to recognize, honor, and be compassionate toward themselves, and to pull themselves back to balance and peace. It is a personal journey with no timeline.

All of us can struggle to be aware of our emotional ups and downs until we learn to recognize them early. We trip along, ignoring the early signs of overwhelm, anxiety, or anger, until those feelings burst forth. Our mind is good at protecting us — it can shut down, run away from, or shove down anything it believes will cause pain. We learn to ignore our body's signals when we are not doing well. Healing requires that we intentionally deal with the trauma that caused the pain.

I learned from my years with horses just how subtle and hidden their signs of stress can be. They may stop chewing or blinking, breathe faster or barely at all. They may raise their heads, tense their muscles, twitch their tails, wrinkle their nostrils or the skin above their eyes, or tighten their lips. They may freeze or run away. It can start with a small widening of the eye or a turn of the head — and it can escalate quickly. I assist my clients in seeing the subtle signs before the horse has to take action.

The love of being with the horse creates a space where the client will hold themselves together for as long as they are able to stay with the horse. I watch carefully, especially if their systems are geared for flight or defense. When clients show signs of stress, before they reach meltdown or explosion, I help them become aware of what is happening in their body. Through that awareness, they learn to diffuse and calm themselves. That is the goal. It takes a lot of practice.

In my adult clients, especially those diagnosed with ASD later in life, I often see emotion turn inward. The explosion becomes internal. I see depression, self-loathing, self-harm, suicidal ideation, and an inability to move in any direction.

Being diligent and paying attention may save us both from becoming reactive. Although I rarely fall into a reactive state, I can have an emotional bump in my road. It's not that I don't react — we all need that fight-or-flight response — but I turn it into, “What should I be doing instead of fleeing?” My ability to regulate myself helps all of us regulate. I stay grounded through proper breathing — long, slow, deep breaths into the belly, fully exhaling before allowing the next breath in — and feeling Mother Earth beneath my feet. I no longer think about the process; I have practiced enough that it is simply part of me. In other words, if I run, you’d better run too.

I was taught to be calm around horses so the horse would remain calm. I am now finding that the horse can co-regulate humans. I teach clients to find calm through slow breaths, focus, intention, presence, and grounding. Horses want to be calm, and they want to be with a calm person. The client wants to be with the horse, so they work on regulating themselves to stay connected. My own self-regulation spreads to both the horse and the client. It is a beautiful triangle of care.

WHEN ALL THE SAFETY PRECAUTIONS IN THE WORLD DON’T WORK

A young boy with Down syndrome who is also on the autism spectrum had been riding with us for several weekly sessions. He was doing well and had learned several of the games we play from the saddle. I intentionally keep the games the same until they are well learned, and then we add to them or change them up a bit. The child had been riding Joe, one of my steadiest ponies — a true team player who knew his role as mentor very well. It was a day when I didn’t have a volunteer to lead the pony. It was just me, both leading and teaching.

Apparently, the boy was tired of the game as he had learned it and decided to get creative. All the careful safety measures I had put in place went down the tubes in a split second. He grabbed the cone instead of the ring that was sitting on a barrel and banged it down hard. I only took my eyes off him for a second to navigate around the barrel. The loud sound startled the pony, who leapt sideways into me, nearly knocking me down. The sideways movement was too much for the young guy, as there was suddenly no pony underneath him. He came off, landing on his bottom in the four inches of sand we have in our arena.

Unfortunately, his elbow hit the rim of the barrel on the way down. It appeared to me that he had badly hurt his elbow. Even though he was nonverbal, I knew at once that he needed to go to the doctor, and I sent him on his way with his dad to urgent care.

My goal is always safety first, and yet horses can and do react swiftly to stimuli. Sometimes there is no way to prepare them for every event that might occur. We build trust as much as possible and hope that trust holds when something scares them. My goal is to have a volunteer for every rider. It's not easy to find them these days. I am so appreciative of the volunteers I have now. They are an additional layer of safety and care we strive for here.

PATTERNS AND FLEXIBILITY

Horses really like patterns. They often take the same path to water; they want their food in the same place at the same time every day. It's easy to teach them new patterns. Each style of riding has different patterns, and while a horse *could* do them all, many have abilities that make them better suited to one area than another. There are speed games like barrel racing and pole bending, all kinds of cattle work, western riding, hunt seat, saddle seat, dressage, jumping indoors and outdoors, cross-country, obstacle courses, reining, racing, and many more. All have a certain amount of pattern to them — some more than others.

I ask my horses to be more mentally and physically flexible than most to build their confidence. My clients sometimes do unexpected things, and the horse needs flexibility of mind to cope with those unexpected changes.

Many of my clients like patterns too. Patterns are predictable, and most are safe. Some of my clients revel in patterns that *aren't* safe, but they are still predictable — even when the outcome isn't always positive. There's a certain kind of comfort in predictability.

I like to teach both patterns and flexibility. We have a simple obstacle course in both our indoor and outdoor areas. The patterns teach how to focus, turn, go, move on a straight line, stop, bend down, cross the midline, plan, and execute the plan. The course has hanging rings which they pull off with alternating hands while in motion, the slowest barrel race in the world, rings to exchange on cones on the barrels, cones to weave through, poles to cross or zigzag, or a jumble of poles to pick their way through. Outside we have a cloverleaf pattern of barrels, a T made of PVC pipe stuck in buckets to exchange rings from (using a figure-eight pattern), a bridge, a tractor tire to cross, logs, a horse-size teeterboard, and a pedestal.

We start with the simpler indoor course to build the pattern for each obstacle, based on the ability and confidence of the rider. I often have them walk the course on the ground with the horse to get a feel for what pattern they need to follow. First, we choose which pattern to walk. When the rider understands how each obstacle is accomplished, then we allow them to choose which one to go to. Eventually, they will give us the whole course pattern they wish to do.

Once a rider is settled into a pattern, I begin to change it. How much I change the pattern depends on the client's level of flexibility. A client who is adamant about things staying the same may do best with only slight tweaks to a game while a more flexible client may be ready for an entirely new game or setup.

For example, we start with the slowest barrel race in the world as a game of its own, walking the barrel pattern. Then, when they are ready to add more — lean over and grab a ring off a cone — I will change the game to cones on the barrels. That game involves picking up a ring from the cone on the first barrel, circling the barrel, going to the next barrel, exchanging rings, turning around that barrel, heading to the third barrel, exchanging rings again, then circling that barrel and returning to the first barrel to place the ring back. It's much more complicated and requires more focus, physical work, mental engagement, and motor planning than the barrel race.

Each obstacle can be changed to a more difficult one by building on increasing skills. The whole game changes again when the rider starts steering the horse by themselves. Then they are not only working with their own bodies and minds — they are working with the horse's body and mind too.

Another way I build flexibility is by introducing variety: riding in different styles of saddles, riding different horses, choosing not to ride and instead working with the horse on the ground, or having a hippology lesson. We have even given the horse a spa day. Before making the decision to change things up, we look for the client's line of tolerance and help them to recognize it as well. I carefully skate along that edge of their tolerance — holding it for a moment or two — to assist them in discovering their capacity for flexibility. We want them to build acceptance of change and be flexible when they need to be.

CHAPTER SEVEN

BEING ONE WITH THE HORSE

"Having respect for animals makes us better humans."

~ Jane Goodall

I was about thirteen years old when my parents bought Flicka and Rick-a-Jay for my younger siblings to ride. The day they came home was the day I became aware of how complicated a horse's thought process could be. The ponies were black Shetlands. Flicka, the mom, was of stocky English breeding and a true stinker. Her son, Rick-a-Jay, was the lighter-boned American type — a sweetie compared to his momma.

Flicka was highly opinionated about how much weight she should have to carry. I was about ten pounds above her limit, and she made that perfectly clear every time I climbed on. I had to ride bareback because the saddle was too small for me. My siblings weren't anywhere near her weight limit, but she needed work on her guidance system — she tended to go wherever she darn well pleased. I accepted the challenge, and the war of wills commenced. If only I knew then what I know now.

She was a smart and conniving little cookie. Every day I would love her and groom her and tell her what a good girl she was. Five minutes later, I would be holding on for dear life as she took off at a fast, tooth-jarring trot, then make a 90-degree turn that left me on my rear end in the field watching her tail disappear in the distance. I walked home a lot that summer. My persistence paid off eventually, and we compromised: I wouldn't ride her anymore, and she wouldn't dump my siblings.

Two more horses soon joined the herd. My mom's horse — a tall Thoroughbred-Quarter Horse named Whiskey — and my Half-Arabian, Karada's Cherokee, moved in and settled well, which led me directly into my next training projects. The next horses I trained were Half-Arabian pinto ponies belonging to my mom's friend. I'm not sure why, but they bred several of them and then didn't do much with them until they wanted them trained. I was brave enough — and uneducated enough — to take on the job. My mom always said I was all guts and no brains. The first two ponies who came to our farm turned out to be easy enough to work with, and their training went great. Success.

Then the owner asked me to work with a mare who was about seven years old and had never been handled. We had to herd her into a stall in their cow barn. It was a small space, about eight-by-eight feet. She was petrified. She was full of burrs, and her mane and tail were twisted into knots. Her eyes were wild with fear. She started to run in that small space, looking for a way out. At one point, she put her head into the corner and cowered. I slipped into the stall with her.

All heck broke loose. She took off running around me. I do not know how I didn't get knocked down and run over. I have no idea how long she ran — it seemed like forever.

Finally, she slowed and stopped, breathing hard and shaking from muzzle to tail. I slowly moved forward and placed my hand on her side. She fell to the floor, then jumped to her feet and ran around again. My tears started to flow, and as soon as I could, I removed myself from the pen. I cried and cried for her. When I could finally talk again, I went to the owner and told them I could never train her

— she was too full of fear to trust me. I never knew what happened to that pretty, wild girl. In my mind, I saw her running free and wild until the end of her days.

That day I learned the lesson of humility — and to honor the horse who shows up. I learned that my loving, gentle manner wasn't enough to help them all. That frightened horse sent me on a journey to learn all I could about communicating with horses. It was a long journey and worth every minute. It may also have been the first time I became aware that it was more important to let her be who she was rather than change her into who I thought she should be. This knowledge has served me well with both clients and horses.

UNDERSTANDING THE HORSE

I grew to be an observer and listener first — and a doer second. I have watched horses in their pastures, while interacting with people, and while escaping and running free like mustangs on the plains. Even after seventy years, I am constantly reminded that I am still a learner.

I experimented for years on how to gently train horses with just enough pressure to get the result I was seeking, but not so much pressure that I got a reaction instead of a response. I never wanted to bully or demand from my beloved horses again. That's how horses were trained in my younger years — at least in my part of the country. The horse was told what to do and was expected to understand and obey. I'm not very obedient either, so I could relate to them. As prey animals, they don't want to be eaten, and they want to flee if they perceive you and your "orders" as threats. I wish I had understood that when I was a young trainer.

It took time, practice, observing, and breaking down my limiting beliefs to get me where I am today. I eventually learned that kindness, caring, and loving patience were better tools than the ones all the "experts" said to use. The only time I get loud and demanding is when I feel I am in danger — and then I get big enough to move them away from me rather than attack them.

I was nearly fifty years old when I discovered the Parelli Natural Horsemanship program. I was skeptical, as I had tried so many professional trainers' methods. I was usually disappointed and found I could pick up a few pointers and leave a lot of what they did in the dust. Natural Horsemanship offered a different perspective on how horses think and different approaches to use with different personalities (Parelli coined the term *Horsenality*).

I found this approach refreshing after the "my cookie-cutter method is better than yours" mentality. I followed the program for several years. All my lesson horses were trained with Natural Horsemanship and my own methods. They are very safe and enjoy their work.

Somewhere along the line, I took a slightly different and more subtle path to training than even the Parelli way. I began asking for more with less and less pressure, and I accepted and respected a "no" when it was given. Once I was in the EGCM two-year program, I was introduced to Melisa Pearce and Carolyn Fitzpatrick's book on horse personalities, *Equusology,* which helped me to develop an even deeper understanding. I found that the more I honor the horses, the more they trust me — and the people with whom we work.

BEGINNING MY WORK WITH HORSES AND CLIENTS

I had been looking for a program model to assist me in my work with children with special needs. I enrolled in PATH (Professional Association of Therapeutic Horsemanship, International) and learned a lot about special needs and how they teach horseback riding. It didn't blend cohesively with how I worked with horses or children. I retained the knowledge I had gained and continued my search. I investigated several other modalities and was never happy with the way the horses were reacting to the activities of the program or how they were asked to respond to the clients. I feel the horse should be happy to be partnered with a human, not feel they need to resist or resent being in the arena. Horses speak very subtly at first, then get bigger when they are ignored. Many of the horses I observed were sending signals of discomfort and, when that didn't work, they started pinning their ears, swishing their tails, or even biting.

I love it when the universe sends me messages in a unique way. I was a member of Spirit Horse Equine Rescue and Education Center and an active Parelli Natural Horsemanship student when the Parellis sponsored a program to train a rescued horse to be auctioned off at the end of the program. Through that program, I met an engaging young man named Robert Goodland, who trained using the Parelli method and was also a student of EGCM. He explained the Gestalt program to the founder and board president of Spirit Horse, DeeDee Golberg. She called me immediately. I was fascinated. The work sounded so much like what I had been searching for that I called Robert right away. He directed me to a woman in my area who was a certified Equine Gestaltist, and I signed up for a session to check it out.

I was awed by the experiential process. I loved the respect and honor given to the horse and the clear message the horse was sending to me. I went home and signed up for an interview to enter the program.

In 2019, I became a student of the Touched by a Horse Equine Gestalt Coaching Method, taught by its founder, Melisa Pearce. Melisa is not only a psychotherapist of many years — she is also a lifelong horsewoman with major accolades for her showing and breeding of horses, as well as stable ownership and wholehearted love of the horse.

Throughout my life, I had learned to shut down the deep and emotionally intuitive parts of me. I was told to buck up, put on my big-girl boots, and deal with it. I was never encouraged to explore the painful areas, to say what needed to be said — or to scream when I needed to scream. I didn't think the program would be able to teach me much more about horses. I was so wrong. I was reawakened to their profound ability to give back. I could once again feel that energy of love and peace they are so gifted at sharing.

I remember that when teenage angst overtook me, I could spend the day with my horses and feel peace and balance again. I always had their support when all else was failing around me. They calmed my sad heart. Then came adulthood, motherhood, divorcehood, and I shut myself off emotionally — no longer allowing my horses to help me. I put my delight and peace with the horse in a box in the corner and ignored it for many years. I continued working with horses, yet I never allowed them to truly help me.

I learned to read body language and sense when I felt unsafe. I avoided feeling what others were feeling because it stirred too much pain in my own body. It felt safer to glide along, untouched by how others were feeling. I wasn't unkind or unsympathetic, just numb. When I began training in EGCM, I knew this was going to have to change. Empathic presence is an important ingredient of Gestalt coaching. I knew I had to find a way to feel what someone else was experiencing — especially when they could not yet find the words. What I didn't know was how to get my empathy back. Our horse, Cotton Candi, showed me the way.

Candi was an amazing little Haflinger with a heart of gold. She had been part of our herd for about ten years and had started many little children on their journey to loving horses. When she was about ten, she developed Squamous Cell Carcinoma in her eyes and had to have the cancer cells frozen off. Later she developed a strange growth in her vaginal area. A couple of years after that, we noticed her eyes looking odd. The veterinarian examined her and said she had cancer inside the eye and recommended removing it. When

I showed him her other end, he shook his head. He believed the cancer was probably all through her body. We canceled the surgery and created a plan to keep her comfortable.

Two weeks later, I came down to the barn to find her in a great deal of pain. It seemed to be coming from her intestinal area. Colic in horses can be anything from a mild gas stomachache to a death sentence. It starts with general discomfort and, depending on the cause, can rapidly send them into decline. They can sweat, roll, look at, or bite their sides. Sometimes the answer is as simple as medication. Sometimes it requires surgery.

I gave Candi the meds we keep on hand when colic starts, called the veterinarian, and walked her in our indoor arena. After a while, she stopped and stood quietly, so I did an acupressure method called the Bladder Meridian to see if I could find the area of pain. As my hand passed over her loin area, a picture popped into my head — a black, roiling mass churning in her intestines. My hands flew away from her body, and I jerked back. I had never envisioned anything like that before. I was completely baffled.

I walked her a little longer to compose myself, then tried again to see if I had imagined it. Again, horrific images appeared in my mind's eye.

Candi was starting to collapse when the vet arrived. We did all we could on the farm. Surgery, given her history, was ill-advised. After discussing her condition, we decided the cancer had likely won, and the most humane act was to euthanize her. My animals stay with me their whole lives, and some live a very long time. Candi did not get to stay as long as we wanted. We will never forget her.

I called Melisa Pearce to help me understand what I had felt and seen. Melisa listened deeply in that beautiful Gestalt way. When I finished my story, she suggested that Candi had given me a gift that day — the gift of sensing what my clients needed to see or say, what my horses were trying to communicate, and the ability to feel again.

My nonverbal clients speak with their energy and their bodies, and I can thank Candi for helping me feel what they want to convey.

ECGM helped me pull together everything I had learned in all my years of searching and practicing into one cohesive program for teaching children with special needs and working with others with emotional and mental-health challenges. We call this Energy Connected Therapeutic Horsemanship.

By combining fifty-seven years of teaching horsemanship, twenty-five years of understanding and teaching early childhood, and four years of deeply learning the Gestalt modality, I developed a powerful way to assist all who come here to find themselves and feel whole.

Our mission is to support people in finding self-awareness, self-compassion, and self-regulation — and with adults, to resolve unfinished business from their past. We believe that everyone is whole, capable, and resourceful in solving their problems, wherever they are on their life's journey.

EGCM training opened my eyes to just how much more the horse brings to the healing process. Research from the HeartMath Institute shows that vibrational energy is scientifically measurable, and that a horse's slow heart rate and breathing can calm and bring a person to a level of peace simply by being present. The horse requires no training for this — it comes naturally — and most are willing to help people who are hurting emotionally and physically.

An article by Diane E. Dreher, PhD, "Why Do Horses Help Us Heal? The promise of equine therapy" (January 6, 2018), states: "Building trust with such a sensitive animal takes time, time that can become a healing, empowering process. For years now, children with a range of issues, including ADHD, autism, eating disorders, abuse, depression, and anxiety, have benefited from equine therapy. The many ways of interacting with a horse — offering it carrots and apples; leading it around on a long line; saddling up and riding it — gradually develop these children's self-awareness and sense of agency. In communicating with a horse, they learn patience, attention, compassion, and responsibility, leading to a greater understanding of themselves and others."[2] The study further concludes that a therapeutic bond with a horse can help foster "mutual trust, respect, affection, empathy, unconditional acceptance, confidence, personal success, responsibility, assertiveness, communication skills, and self-control."[3]

I work with my horses to trust humans, even though they see us as predators and themselves as prey. From the first day they come to the farm, they are respected for their opinions and individuality. It may take up to two years for them to understand that they can say no and be respected for that answer.

Most horses are trained to obey. I approach a horse with respect and offer the back of my hand. If they reach forward and touch my hand, I know I have been cleared for contact. If they turn away, I turn away and wait until I am approached. When I start to work with them, I suggest that they try something my way and then wait for their answer. If the horse has no prior training, I may suggest it again at the same level of polite curiosity. If the horse is being retrained, I may add a tiny bit of pressure — an ask, not a demand. I rarely add any more pressure than that.

I stay soft, slow, and calm. I want to trigger curiosity rather than fear. Horses never forget when they've been hurt or forced. It creates a host of training pitfalls. I watch for any signs of fear — pinched or flared nostrils, wide eyes, wrinkles above the eyes, faster or shallow breathing, tight lips, ears back, tail twitching, restlessness. The faster I see any change from relaxation, the faster I can back off and give

---

[2] Diane E. Dreher, "Why Do Horses Help Us Heal? The Promise of Equine Therapy," *Psychology Today*, January 6, 2018.

[3] E. Q. Rothe et al., "From Kids and Horses: Equine-Facilitated Psychotherapy for Children," *International Journal of Clinical and Health Psychology* 5 (2005): 373–383, esp. 376.

them time to return to curiosity. A horse — and a human — cannot learn when they have slipped into fear. They can only learn in curiosity. When pushed too fast, they switch to flight responses, and I must go back a few steps to regain trust and curiosity.

I have worked with several rescued horses. They often need a lot of time to adjust to a kinder home. I have also had horses who came from good homes but took a long time to adjust to a place where they are allowed to say no. And when they say yes, it's a big deal.

We have been working with a fourteen-year-old gaited mare who was sweet and kind and knew very little about riding. She could be led anywhere but wouldn't move if the lead line was removed. We've been teaching her the "bucket game" through positive reinforcement. This past week, I climbed on without a bridle or even a halter, and we played together. With a little help from our instructor, she went from bucket to bucket in search of her six little timothy pellets, calm and eager. This was so much sweeter than using pressure to move her from one place to another.

My training methods continue at this slow pace of waiting for acceptance at each step of being trained to ride and work with all kinds of riders. I have found that once they accept that they are respected and have a right to say no, they rarely say no. My horses come to me in the fields when I carry halters. They rarely refuse to come — or worse, walk away. If they do, I go find someone else who wants to come play.

CHAPTER EIGHT

COMBINING ALL INTO PARTNERSHIP

"There needs to be more emphasis on what a child can do instead of what they cannot do."

~ Dr. Temple Grandin

I am often asked, *Why horses?* Horses are amazing at calming us and teaching us to breathe, relax, and feel more present. My experience with them has taught me to trust what they are telling me about the client. A horse may stay close, touching the client often. Where they touch also tells me where the emotional or physical pain is located. I use this information to form a plan to assist the client.

For clients who are riding, I listen to the horse's reaction to their rider. I am looking for avenues to break through to the inner person, helping them open to trust both the horse and me. I find that self-regulation is a huge challenge for many of my ASD, ADD, and ADHD clients. A client cannot learn when they are sitting in fear. The horse is a master of emotional resonance, sending calming vibrational energy that soothes fear and opens the door to learning.

Our method of teaching clients how to interact with the horse helps bring self-regulation, self-awareness, and self-compassion into play. Clients often say that when they experience dysregulation, their bodies simply take over and they have no control over their emotions. Working with the horses — using their own energy to move, turn, and stop — helps them understand how they can have control not only of the horse but of themselves as well.

We teach them to use body movements and to read the horse's body to understand its emotions. This developed awareness naturally extends to recognizing the body language of people too. We work on focus and intention, teaching them to direct their energy toward a target and release it upon arrival. Imagine the power of that awakening for someone who feels they cannot control themselves. We often say *less is more*. That approach suits our riders well as they guide a thousand-pound horse with quiet, soft, intentional movements in a pattern that works for them.

We get them interested in the horse's life and history. We teach them to connect their hearts to the horses, to understand how the horse thinks and feels. When they begin to understand, they begin to empathize, and with empathy they begin to connect to the animals and the people around them. They begin to feel the energy that flows from one being to another.

ENERGY

Melisa Pearce has a wonderful way of helping us see energy in a natural, scientific way. She explains how molecules in steel are moving even though we do not notice the movement. The energy of all things moves all the time. We, as humans, are no different. We vibrate at a different speed than other things in our environment, and horses vibrate at a higher level than we do. Their desire to keep the herd at a high vibrational level is how they help humans feel better. Like tuning forks, they resonate to bring our vibrational level up to theirs. Energy is never lost or destroyed; instead, it can be converted or tuned up.

Through years of practice, observing, and being with animals, I have developed a feel for where an animal's or a person's energy level is sitting. This is important for how I interact with them — which horse I partner them with, and what expectations to set for the session. This can change each time I meet them. Not only do clients have their own innate natural level, but their environment, anxiety, anticipation, past and present experiences, and daily challenges can shift how I need to meet them in that moment.

When I find their energy level, I determine whether it is their natural state or whether it is due to being here with the horses. I know my horses well and match the child with a horse who can help calm them or match them at their energy level. The choice depends on the personality of the client. If I feel the "buzz" is from fear, I choose a horse who can tolerate the fear and reassure the client that they are in good hooves.

I bring into the mix the ability to regulate my own energy and vibrational level. Through my calmness, I can co-regulate the horse, and together we help the client regulate. I am working toward curiosity and regulation, self-awareness, and eventually the ability to bring energy up or down at will — up energy to get the horse to go and down energy to stop. When the client finds that spark of courage and curiosity they never knew they had, they grow in leaps and bounds.

If the buzzing vibration is a natural state for the client, I choose a horse with good sensory input (a bit bumpy) and a fun, safe attitude. The client learns how to shut their energy down to stop and regulate it to go — and how fast.

When the client's energy level is very low and sluggish, it is a different set of decisions. A new client with low energy will be matched with an easygoing, slower-moving horse. As the client feels safe and trust is built, I will choose a new partner who requires them to bring up their energy level to get the horse to go.

I adjust my own energy to match or complement the client. When I sense fear or anxiety, I project peace, calm, and confidence in what we will be doing together. I breathe quietly, slowly, and deeply like a horse. I slow everything down. I want the client to stay curious and ready to learn, not slide deeper into fear. I match them with my calmest horse to begin building a partnership. The horse needs to project inner peace and empathy to envelop the client and help them feel safe.

Fear is a tough emotion for all my clients, whether they are typically developing or have special needs. Once anxiety sets in — whether from experience or imagination — it is hard to turn around. I am careful and clear with my safety instructions. A horse can inadvertently cause injury, and it is usually the person's lack of education or awareness that gets them hurt. I want them to watch and be aware of what the horse is aware of and why they do what they do. It is rare here for a horse to hurt a human, and almost never on purpose.

We did have one incident where a child was nipped by a mare because the child was crabby and a bit pushy. The mare was a momma and nipped her the way she would have corrected her own filly. She has never done it again. The incident brought fear into the girl, and it took a few sessions — and talking about what happened and why — to rebuild trust. It was a powerful lesson in partnership.

If I sense "the need for speed" or a need for sensory input, I go all out for fun and activity. I keep the pace a bit faster for as long as the client can stay regulated without skipping essential safety and health considerations.

I see energy as a continuum, as changeable as the weather here in Wisconsin. Many things influence energy: the environment, personalities, weather, sensory issues, new or old experiences, how school went that day, even the car ride to the farm. The atmosphere at That Zen Farm is truly Zen-like. The teachers, volunteers, horses, arena, and lounge are all calm and ready to serve the needs of the clients. Our ability to regulate ourselves helps the client regulate themselves.

I work to build a partnership between the client and one horse until the client understands the basics. When I see confidence and curiosity about a new horse, I change it up. The horses here are very good at supporting the clients, and they look to me to see whether the energy is for forward movement or whether the client is unregulated. My lack of engagement keeps the horse focused on settling the client. When I add my energy to the mix, the horse responds with forward movement based on my energy. The horses are connected to me as well as the client and will follow my energy lead.

We strive to eventually hand the reins to the rider, slowly allowing them to make more decisions and take control. Our goal is to see them ride independently. While some never get there, many do — and it is a joy every time.

TRUST BUILDING

I build trust into the horse-client relationship in many ways. One way is to help the client understand why the horse does what he does, how his brain is wired, and what to expect. Horses have a high flight response to stimuli. A well-trained and trusting horse may only flinch or shudder when something unexpected happens. Even a steady horse can have an unexpected reaction. In our arena, we have sidewalls about five feet high to keep the horses from accidentally kicking through the steel walls. Sometimes a safety measure can backfire in unusual ways.

One day our sweet Haflinger, Naughty John, was quietly walking along with a young rider while I led him, when a cat leapt up from the back side of the wall right into John's face. John jumped sideways a couple of feet, unseating his rider and stepping on me. After giving the cat an evil side-eye glance and blowing out his breath, John allowed his rider to remount and walked on. He kept a close eye on that place for several months, though. The child riding him that day had a momentary setback in her trust. We worked through it by helping her understand that the horse felt he was in danger. We asked how it feels to feel unsafe and what she would do if faced with that fear. We talked about how horses have a built-in release system to calm down and return to a neutral state.

Building trust is one of my highest priorities. As much as I would like them to be, horses are not one hundred percent predictable. They are flight animals and, no matter how well trained they are, they will react to unexpected stimuli. If a horse cannot see what is coming, hears an unfamiliar noise, or something suddenly appears in their view, it will react — sometimes with a subtle body shudder, sometimes with full flight. For this reason, the horse must trust that I am keeping them safe. That means I must be fully grounded and able to absorb whatever shows up in our work area. At the same time, I am asking my client to trust that I will keep them safe while they are working with an unfamiliar experience and a large animal. My horses weigh between nine hundred and two thousand two hundred pounds. That is asking for a lot of trust.

When a client grooms the horse, I find it is a great way to make a connection the horse can understand. They enjoy having someone scratch those hard-to-reach bug bites. Herds of horses generally move together toward food, water, and a safe place to sleep. We strive to instill in the client that a good human partner knows where they want to go, focuses on that destination, stays calm and present, and never hurts the horse. These are all things horses understand as part of a trusting relationship.

One of our newer clients, who is neurodivergent and nonverbal, was petrified at her first meeting with Billy Bob, a Haflinger who weighs around nine hundred pounds. He is as sweet and quiet as they come. She was so frightened that she had to stay on one side of the corral panel and Billy on the other. Her steadfast father worked with her for almost forty-five minutes before she was able to pet the horse on the forehead by herself.

Over the next three weeks, she learned to brush and lead. On her third lesson, I asked if she wanted to ride. I showed her how to mount, and she climbed right up. We did a little walking on Billy that day and declared a victory. On the fourth week, she had the routine down and almost climbed on before I had the girth tightened. With her dad on one side, me on the other, and a volunteer leading Billy, we set off on the day's horse adventure.

We worked the obstacle course for the first time that lesson — going around three barrels (in the slowest barrel race in the world) and through the horse wash (pool noodles suspended from a bar over the riding path), then pulling down rings suspended overhead. She rode for twenty minutes, which is a lot of sensory input for a new horse girl. She signed that she was done, and we walked back to the mounting block where she dismounted beautifully. As we were walking back to the saddling area, she reached over, grabbed my hand, and laced her fingers in mine. My heart soared. I felt I had made a new friend and opened her world to the magic of the horse. Her dad stepped back and let her be with me to take the tack off, brush Billy, and give him his cookie treat in a bucket.

I want my clients to trust that I will not ask them to do the impossible, and yet I will stretch them to the next level. I wait until I feel they are ready — or when they express that they are ready. I do have a few who feel ready before I think they are, and I let them try to soar when I can.

SAFETY

That Zen Farm strives for the safest experience we can possibly arrange. As I mentioned before, horses are not one hundred percent predictable. They are flight animals and will resort to flight if they feel threatened. We work hard to get our horses comfortable with many different stimuli — children who scream in excitement, sudden unexpected movements, noises outside the arena, unbalanced riders, and whatever else I can think of to help the horses be steady and calm.

They can still be reactive, and we build in safety by having a knowledgeable horse leader to help the horse cope without running away as instinct tells them to do. While training the horses, we gently work toward acclimating them to stimuli (scary things). We find the line where curiosity may tip into fear and then praise (reward) and retreat to a safer place as defined by the horse. We do not punish natural responses. When they do react, we go back a couple of training steps, find the hole in their training, and start again.

When a new client starts, we first teach them to yell "Door!" before they enter the arena. This gives the horses and the people inside a heads-up that someone is entering. We spend time teaching about the areas of the horse that can be dangerous. We show them what a horse might look like if they are getting upset with the client or another horse. Horses give subtle cues that are often out of our awareness. Learning what a calm or on-alert horse looks like can save us from unexpected dangerous reactions. We stop what we are doing to create a teachable moment. Of course, if we need to remove the rider from the saddle or the arena, we do that first.

We reinforce good habits, like making sure the horse always knows where we are. Horses cannot see directly in front of them or directly behind, and they can be surprised if you pass under their neck and pop up suddenly on the other side. We teach clients to place a hand on the horse's hindquarter and say, "Coming around." If they are unable to give a verbal warning, we do it for them. We have them walk close to the hind legs or far around, out of reach of those long hind legs. The strongest part of the kick is at the end of the kick. Every part of our on-the-ground and in-the-saddle program works toward safe interactions.

FOCUS AND INTENTION

I have realized that horses like to know where they are going. Some wild-herd observers say that herd members look to the leader to make decisions about when to go to water, where to find food, and where to go next. As humans, we also need to know where we are going. It is hard to get anything done if you are aimlessly wandering, either mentally or physically.

When teaching how to get a horse to go where we want it to move, I have found that we need focus and intention. This can be much harder than it sounds. Whether you are a special-needs or typically developing person, concentration is a fleeting thing. And that is okay. We refocus and refocus and refocus until we reach our destination.

To teach this concept, I have the client pick a place to go that is straight ahead and close. Then they make an intention — out loud is best, because then we as helpers can hear it too. We have horse leaders with many of our clients so they are not run down or squished against a wall. The client says something like, "I intend to walk to the orange cone and stop." Then we pick the next spot and the next intention. If they cannot verbalize the destination, I ask them to point to it.

RUN A MOVIE (VISUALIZATION)

I have always known that horses pick up cues from me that I have not put into physical form. The more I recognized that they "read my mind," the more I looked for ways to help clients use mental imagery rather than relying solely on physical cues. Through trial and error, I found that the best way for clients to learn this concept was to give them context from their daily lives.

Most of my clients have access to online games and movies. Therefore, while working with the horses, we add "run a movie" to the focus and intention. This part is simple for my visual learners — they can send a mental video of their focus and intention with little effort. Other learning styles may take longer unless I can connect the idea to their favorite video games. I ask them to see themselves and the horse going to the place of intention as though they were in a game. If they cannot do that, we ask them simply to look where they intend to go.

I have noticed a difference in my clients as this concept of planning and sending their energy ahead of them takes hold. They wander less and walk taller, moving with intention toward their next place. And then it starts happening even without a horse. I love seeing the transformation from hiding in their hoodies to striding into the arena ready to work with a horse.

A neurodivergent young man who came to That Zen Farm walked in with his head down, buried in his hoodie, dragging his toes through the sand. He had suffered many insults from others because of his large size and his differences. I felt that defeat of spirit clear through me. We talked about looking and acting like a victim. We practiced walking with confidence — both with the horse and alone. We worked on meeting the gaze of another person without flinching. We worked on *being-ness* — learning to be in a space, in a place, and to own the space where he was.

It took months to break the pattern of hiding his light. And when the light started to shine through, so did his amazing personality and confidence. He now walks tall and proud and no longer looks like someone you could easily bully.

SEND YOUR ENERGY

When focus, intention, and "run a movie" are understood, we add "send your energy." If you think of your center — the belly-button area — as the source of your "go power," it becomes the burst of energy that sends you off to speed down the track. Some clients find controlling their energy easier than others. Some people have a buzz of energy all the time. For them, learning to dial it down and send it in a focused direction is the first task. Others have a slow-burning energy, which horses generally enjoy being next to. Horses would rather graze on grass, drink water, and take naps than be ridden any day. They enjoy the easygoing nature of these people, but it is more difficult to get from point A to point B.

When we want the horse to halt, we shut that energy off and go into a neutral position. When walking with a horse, I ask the client to exhale slowly with a slight sound; when their breath is gone, they stop their feet and relax. When they are astride the horse, it is the same — exhale, settle a bit deeper into the saddle (not slumping), and enter a neutral state of energy. The automatic relaxation after a deep sigh is a big signal to the horse to relax and breathe too.

GROWING SELF-AWARENESS AND SELF-COMPASSION

As an Equine Gestaltist, my job is to assist clients in finding wholeness in themselves and becoming comfortable with who they are. Even though children are still growing and changing, we strive for them to become more aware of what they are feeling, how to deal with those emotions, and how to be compassionate toward themselves. We connect self-awareness to awareness outside of themselves — first with the horse, then with the world around them, and finally with other people.

Creating Emotional Connections

One of our goals is to find a way to connect the client to the horse and then broaden that connection to people. Emotions are hard for many of my clients. They feel they have anger, fear, anxiety, and sadness. It is hard for them to see that they also have balancing emotions — and often no awareness of them.

I often start by teaching them how the horse expresses fear and helping them make a connection to how *they* feel when they are afraid. We explore what the horse's body language looks like when the horse is expressing happiness — such as finding that perfect itchy place and scratching it for them. I ask questions about how the client feels and where they feel those same emotions in their own body. I acknowledge emotions when I see them occurring so they can become more aware of when they arise. When I hear "I don't know," it is often the truth — they genuinely do not know.

One client insisted he had no hobbies that gave him pleasure. He was surprised to discover that he was actually experiencing joy when he played guitar, composed music, designed and built useful things on a three-dimensional printer, and built furniture and cabinets. He did not know those activities were enjoyable until we explored what joy might feel like.

Another young man's go-to was finding the negative side of every event in his life. We spent many visits figuring out the upside of those events — what he gained by going through them and what he felt when he found the shiny bits. It took months of work before he could give me both sides of an emotional event. He still sees the negative first, and then his self-awareness kicks in and he finds the positive side. Maybe one day the positive will be his go-to.

Finding Empathy

I feel empathy is inside all of us, even if it is buried deep. I find that even my neurotypical clients can have trouble walking in someone else's shoes, feeling what the other person may be feeling. Those clients who are full of self-preservation have trouble allowing themselves to feel what others are feeling. They have enough to deal with inside themselves — their own energy and emotions. They do not want to connect or feel anyone else's.

I often start with having empathy for the horse. I teach clients to read the horse's body language and auditory cues. We work on what those signals could mean to the horse. We experiment and experience ways to understand and connect with what the horse might be feeling. Allowing oneself to feel and find the emotions attached to body language is an inexact science and a guessing game. Horses cannot talk, and the only way to know if you have solved their problem is to reread what they are saying with their bodies — and sometimes guess again.

One of the simplest examples I give is grooming. A horse can show in many ways whether being curried or brushed is comforting and connecting, or annoying and possibly painful. The horse might start by moving away from the grooming tool, twitching their tail, pursing their lips, or showing worry lines above their eyes. If ignored, the body language might get louder — swinging their body away, pinning their ears, biting the air or the person, stomping a foot, or even kicking. I do not let it get to those latter stages because I do not want the horse irritated or the client hurt. I ask clients to watch for the signs, try different pressure, and experiment with different speeds to see if they can help the horse relax and enjoy the grooming process.

This practice of watching how the horse is processing assists my clients in seeing the subtle changes in their own bodies when things are not going well.

Connecting to the Outside World

One of my main goals is to assist clients in creating pathways to greet the outside world. When a person is stuck in their head, they are less likely to make a strong connection to the horse. Horses want us to live in our hearts and emotional selves, as they do not have logic centers in their brains. They observe, feel, and react to their world. Yet they rarely act in anger — which I believe is actually rooted in fear.

Fear can come from humans being harsh in their attitudes toward horses in general, in husbandry practices (feeding or not feeding, moving horses from one place to another, sheltering, veterinary work, hoof care), in training styles, or even from traumatic events unrelated to humans. Sadly, some of my clients' fears come from these same places. It is how we treat one another.

Horses have a great feel for when a client is in distress. They find where the client is hurting and will place their heads or bodies in alignment with the area of pain. They bring peace to the client in a way that is beautiful to behold. I assist in bringing awareness to what the client is feeling and help them find a way to connect to the outer world.

What would it be like to interact with other people and feel this peaceful? What would it take to find that peace again? How can the client pull up that peace so they can interact with others without the pain of the past interfering? What would it be like to sit and talk with others without fear, defensiveness, or anger?

Being with a horse requires the client to pay attention to their surroundings so they are aware of what the horse sees and hears. The horse is going to react to something it does not understand, and the client needs to pay attention to that. They need to be ready to steady and co-regulate through deep, slow breathing and blowing out their breath. They might even need to be ready to move out of the way. When a client is with the horse, they need to stay grounded and present to keep themselves safe. And when they discover they can help regulate the horse, they may also find they can regulate themselves.

That self-regulation can then help them in places of discomfort, allowing them to meet the outside world on their own terms.

The pure joy — and the creation of new neural pathways in the brain — connects the rider to the horse and to the outer, real world. Riding a horse is bliss in movement.

ENERGY CONNECTED THERAPEUTIC HORSEMANSHIP PROGRAM

That Zen Farm's Energy Connected Therapeutic Horsemanship program brings all of these concepts — energy, intention, trust, empathy, and emotional regulation — into a structured, hand-son experience with the horse. This is where clients begin to practice, in real time, the skills that help them grow both inside and outside the arena. Many of the children and teens who come to That Zen Farm are supported through state or county Health and Human Services programs, making this work accessible to families who might otherwise never have the opportunity. If you are seeking similar support, check with your local Health and Human Services office to explore whether financial assistance for equine therapy is available. What unfolds here is far more than a riding lesson; it is a guided partnership that nurtures confidence, connection, and the discovery of one's own inner strength.

The Horsemanship Lesson

Each time a client enters the arena, I have them greet the horse with an extension of their hand toward the horse's nose. I have them offer the back of the hand so the horse does not think there is a treat attached to the greeting. We look for signs of concern — from both the horse and the human. I am feeling into the energy coming from each of them. I am looking for connection or the lack of it. We talk about safety first. Then I teach the bank robber's knot. I firmly believe in a quick-release knot whenever I need to tie a horse. Most of my horses will stand for grooming and saddling without being tied, as they enjoy their work.

We start grooming with a curry comb. The client offers it to the horse to smell, seeking permission to continue. The horse has a choice to sniff the curry comb or turn its head away. If the horse turns away — a sign that they cannot or do not want to work with a person in that moment — I will change horses if possible. If permission is granted, the client begins at the top of the neck, under the mane, using a circular motion to bring the dirt up from near the skin to the surface. We do not use the curry on the face or below the muscled areas of the legs. We do use shedding blades during the spring shed or if the horse has a lot of dried mud on its body.

I encourage the client to use both left and right hands while grooming. My horses generally enjoy being groomed — it is how they build relationships with their herd mates and with their human partners. I have the client try different pressures and different speeds to see if they can help the horse feel comfortable and enjoy the process. Some people need to be taught how to apply pressure differently from their natural mode. A lot of this has to do with their own sensory input-output system.

When changing sides of the horse, I remind clients that the horse has blind spots in its very wide vision range. One is under the nose and neck, one is on top of the back, and the other is directly behind. When we want to move to the other side, we place one hand on the horse's haunch — the thigh area — and say, "Coming around." We walk close to the hind legs, trailing our hand around the horse's buttocks to the other side. If the horse were to kick out, walking close may cause the person to be pushed aside rather than struck. If a person is farther away, they will receive the hardest punch of the kick. If walking close to the back legs is too uncomfortable for the client, I tell them to go way around — but still let the horse know where they are.

When the currying is done, we get the stiff brush and use a push-flick method of grooming, following the natural growth of the hair coat. Here again, I ask clients to pay attention to the horse's reaction to their pressure and speed. Are they satisfying the horse's need to be groomed by a friend, or are they annoying the horse? Is the horse moving away from the pressure or leaning into it? Is the horse calm or agitated? What can they do to shift the horse's attitude to a better one?

There are a couple of grooming areas where I wait until clients are more competent and confident — and in some cases, strong enough — to do the job. I clean the horse's hooves until I feel they can be confident and safe doing it. Some clients can do it fairly soon, and some never do. We also do not brush manes and tails during lessons because the thick hair my horses have makes it too time-consuming. We save that for bath days when it is too hot to ride but they still want to play with horses. We call it a spa day.

When the client is new, I choose whether to use the bareback pad, the all-purpose English saddle, or the western saddle. I evaluate the rider for core strength, balance, flexibility, and confidence. I like to start riders on the bareback pad. They must use their own balance and core strength rather than rely on the saddle to hold them in place, as there are no stirrups to push against or saddle horn to hold. I find they feel the horse better, the horse gives them feedback more quickly, and the horse's motion translates to the client's brain-body connection more efficiently. The bareback pad offers huge sensory input, which can be overwhelming and must be monitored closely. Clients work much harder and get tired or overstimulated much faster than when in a saddle.

If the client is less sure or needs time to build core strength and balance, I use the English saddle. The horse can still feel them, and they can feel the horse, and they have stirrups to support their feet and a more solid seat for security. If the client is top-heavy and very unbalanced, I start them in a western saddle. I do not allow them to grab the horn for support, as it pulls them forward and off balance.

The weight of the rider is distributed over a larger area, which helps the horse balance the client and feels better to the horse as well.

When we get the balance and strength issues corrected and the rider's core is built up, I will try different saddles. I believe this helps break the tendency to want only one pattern and builds flexibility. When they have had a taste of all the styles, I often ask what they want to ride in. I may make the call myself if I have a plan and need to be sure they are safe. One of those projects is riding the outdoor obstacle course. There are hills and objects the horse climbs up and down, and the client may need a saddle to help keep them on board when they are having trouble communicating with their bodies about where their body is in space when navigating the obstacle.

We use air-filled pads under our saddles. I teach each client the importance of handling the pad carefully and not dropping it, as the inner cells cannot be fixed if they get sand in the valve. I also tell them that I am the only one who has dropped them — which is pretty much true. I stay close and allow them to be in charge of the care of the pad. I do not impose consequences if they drop it, and it is a rare occurrence when it does hit the ground. The pad is lighter than the saddle, and it is a good way for them to practice our method of putting saddles on until they are skilled enough, tall enough, and strong enough to put the saddle on.

As with the curry and the brush, we offer the pad to the horse to sniff. If the horse turns their head away or moves away, I bring a different horse. I truly feel the horse must be a willing partner in the session each and every time we work with a client. I would not force a client to be a partner if they did not feel up to it. Horses can feel off, unwell, or unwilling just as easily as people. They "speak" with very small, subtle cues, and we, as their interpreters, must be aware of them.

We tighten the girth only enough to keep the saddle from slipping. The client learns that their hand should slide easily between the girth and the horse down by the horse's elbow. We will tighten the girth or cinch two more times before the riding begins.

Bridling

We do not use bits in our horses' mouths. We use bitless bridles in a variety of styles to suit each horse's individual taste and needs. We usually leave the halter on with the lead rope so the volunteer has what we call "the emergency brake." I want the client to understand that they have control to the best of their ability, and volunteers are only there to help when absolutely needed.

The client is asked to put on their helmet and find the horse's bridle. Each horse has a specific bridle, and the client learns which one belongs to their partner.

When bridling, the client stands facing forward on the left side next to the horse's head and slides the reins over the horse's neck. I use a single soft rope rein that is about ten feet long, clipped to each side of the bridle. It saves on tying knots in single reins or having reins dropped. The rope also works better for clients with sensory issues than leather or stiffer rope.

Then I have them hold the crown of the bridle in their right hand and the chin strap (if there is one) in the other hand. My horses are trained to lower their heads into the bridle. The client then rotates one ear forward into the crown and then the other, making sure the crown sits behind the back of the ear and the browband rests just below the ear. The client then secures the throatlatch. Most of mine have a buckle, and that is often a new experience for younger clients. We explain that the throatlatch is a safety device and must be properly buckled. We fasten it so that at least three fingers can fit upright between the strap and the gullet where the trachea and esophagus are.

I teach clients that horses need reassurance and feedback to know when they are doing their job properly. The horses see many clients during the week, and each person uses energy in their own unique way. To help the horse understand the person's way of saying go, stop, or turn, the person needs to let the horse know when they get it right. I ask the client to stroke the horse's neck three or four times and say "good boy" or "good girl" while the horse is doing the correct thing.

We then pull the safety knot out (or hand the lead to the child) so they can practice walking, halting, and turning. The volunteer is either holding the end of the lead line or standing on the far side from the child holding the reins. We use nine- or ten-foot lead lines so there is plenty to work with and crowding is not an issue. The client holds one hand about a foot from the snap on the halter, then folds the remaining rope in half and holds it with the opposite hand to avoid tripping over it or having the horse step on it. We are careful that the rope is never in a circle or near the client's neck in case the horse feels the need to flee.

My horses are used to a lot of things but have on occasion run from snow sliding off the roof, a loud crack of thunder or lightning, or a strange sound. Recently, a man on a recumbent bicycle drove by on the highway and totally startled one of my newer horses. He still feels the need to go down to the gate and check the road to make sure it is not there again. I find my horses are braver when they are out in the weather rather than tucked nicely into a warm, dry arena.

I ask clients not to pull or drag their new friend around the arena. I explain that this is their new partner and they should walk this journey together. They stand in the mid-neck area so they can see the horse's head and where the horse is looking. This is part of the safety plan. If the client cannot see where the horse's attention is, they cannot be prepared for what might happen next.

To start, we ask the client to pick a spot to walk to (or we choose one for them) that is not more than fifteen to twenty feet away. We ask them to look at the spot, run a movie in their head about going to that spot, bring their energy up like the feeling when someone says "ready, set, go," and start walking. Most of the time, the horse will follow along. If this does not happen, I have them stop, refocus, reset their intention, and try again. If the horse still does not follow, I have them march in place to bring the horse's energy up and encourage the horse to want to follow. I ask them to start slowly, matching the horse, and then finish their walk. When walking clockwise, the client walks on the right side of the horse; when going counterclockwise, they walk on the left.

One of the interesting things I have discovered is that neurodivergent clients often understand the process of "running a movie" and can accomplish it much faster than neurotypical clients. Temple Grandin may have the answer when she says many on the spectrum think in pictures — as horses do. I know it is possible for both to succeed when they can keep the image front and center.

When they arrive at their destination, I have the client exhale with an audible sound. The horse can hear the exhalation, and the client's body will automatically begin relaxing. When their breath is gone, they stop their feet and shut off their energy. Most of the horses are listening for that exhale, and when they hear it, they stop right there. If the horse continues to walk and the client has stopped, the horse will bump into the halter and stop himself. We continue this exercise until the client has figured it out and the horse has an idea of what the client sounds and feels like when they are asking for a stop. I have the client pet the horse after each stop, as I feel that a good stop makes a great partnership. This is also when we tighten the girth another notch — not completely tight.

We work on stopping and starting until the client is mostly comfortable, and then we move to turning. If they are on the left-hand side of the horse, we teach them to turn left first. I have them turn their head and look in the direction they want to go, then turn their torso, then step off in that direction. The horse generally follows without pulling on the lead line or needing additional cues. If the horse does need more information, we have the client gently, softly, calmly add a little pressure to the lead line and wait until the horse takes a step in the proper direction.

I sometimes ask them to pretend they have a laser light coming from their belly button, shining in the direction they want to go. I find that many clients who shuffle along looking at their feet suddenly find a new way of walking and presenting themselves to the world. They now have focus, intention, and a goal — plus the energy to get there. How cool is that.

If we have time, we walk through our simple indoor obstacle course. We have noodles hanging from a pole across the path. We call this a car wash or a pony wash. This is a sensory challenge for some clients — and in the beginning, for the horse too.

Mounting

We use a wooden four-step mounting block that is about three feet wide. We do not have handrails, as we use volunteers to assist those who need help going up and down the steps. This usually changes as the client gains balance, strength, and confidence on their journey.

We have the client walk the horse to the mounting block and stop before the horse is lined up for mounting. We close the valve on the saddle pad, tighten the girth (or cinch), and set the stirrups, guessing at the appropriate length. Once a client is a regular, we try to remember their stirrup number so it is all set when they get on. We usually go with a stirrup at about ankle height to give the rider better stability.

In the beginning, we line the horse up for mounting, asking the client to wait until we say the horse is in the best place and ready for the rider to mount. They quickly learn to line the horse up by themselves. We use a verbal "step up" and a hand gesture for the horse to follow. If the horse is having trouble lining up, we ask the front end to move closer to the block by placing our fingertips on the muzzle and the other hand behind the elbow on the ribs, adding energy (not actual pressure) to move the front end over. To move the hind end, we raise our hand up and out to the side, adding energy by gently bouncing our hand as though bouncing a ball near the hindquarters. We gently rub the horse when they move into place. Lots of love for the effort to understand what we want. We teach our horses to be mounted on both sides in case we have a client who is weaker on one side than the other.

When the horse is in place, we give permission to get on. We help those who need help and encourage those who can but are unsure. We encourage the client to put a foot in the stirrup, place both hands on the pommel, and swing the other leg over the horse's rump, sitting down gently. We hand them the reins and adjust the stirrups to ankle length (a bit longer for western riders). We tighten the girth or cinch if needed and get ready to ride. My heart opens wide when I see the happy smile spreading across the child's face. We wait for a moment so the horse and rider learn to pause; otherwise, a pattern of going can take over before everyone is ready, which could become a safety issue.

Riding

I teach a balanced seat. The rider sits tall without tension, imagining a string attached to the top of their helmet gently pulling them upright but not tight. They slightly tuck their tailbone under, riding on their "back pockets." There should be a plumb line running from their ear straight down to the elbow, down to the back of the leg, and to the ground. Toes should be slightly up. Eyes are soft and level, focused in the direction they want to go. There should be softness in the back, hips, knees, and ankles. Once they are moving, they allow their lower body to follow the motion of the horse.

Once the volunteers, horse, rider, and teacher are ready, we let the rider know that the volunteer holding the lead line is the emergency brake, and any other volunteers are for safety. The rider is in charge, and when they are ready, they choose a nearby destination. I start with a target maybe twenty feet away. My walls have letters, unicorns, and rainbows, and the arena has many obstacles that can be used as destinations. I ask them to look at the object, decide that is where they want to go, run a movie of the pair of them going there, then bring up their energy ("ready, set, go!") and send all of that mentally toward the destination.

If they are successful, the horse moves forward. If the horse does not understand, we have them tic-toc their shoulders to gently engage their seat bones and send a rhythm to the horse's spine. If after four or five tic-tocs the horse is still standing still, we have the rider close their whole leg — from hip to ankle — against the horse. If this still does not work, we start over. I explain that the horse is not understanding what they are saying, and instead of getting bigger, we are going to get softer and wait longer between asks.

There is a certain amount of frustration when the horse is unresponsive to cues. I allow for this to a point and then give a little help. I want to build problem-solving, the ability to feel frustration and recover from it, and the confidence and competency to get the job done through good energy and effort. I am always analyzing where the moment is — where the line sits before it crosses from frustration into anger. For some clients, it is a short trip, and I must watch so they feel the frustration but are not overwhelmed by it. It is not about pushing them; it is about focus, intention, exploration, self-awareness, and then self-regulation. The pure joy on their faces when the horse walks brightens my day too.

Many of the clients I work with have trouble with low muscle tone and weak core strength. The act of sitting up can be a major skill to learn. We want them tall but not tight. Imagining a string tied to the top of their helmet gently pulling upward helps straighten the spine without creating a hollow in the lower back. We do not expect them to maintain this position for long. Gentle reminders are used, and if they allow touch, we place a soft hand in the center of their back. Riding is all about core use. It keeps the rider balanced, allows the horse and rider to move as one, and is used for turning, controlling, and stopping. The rider is encouraged to do as much as they can for as long as they can.

When we reach the destination, we ask them to exhale with a sigh, relax their body, and settle into the saddle without slumping. The exhale relaxes the body and shuts off the energy directed at the horse. If the horse does not stop after a count of four, we add one rein raised straight up with a straightened elbow. If this does not work, the volunteer exhales and stops their feet, allowing the horse to bump into the halter. We call this the emergency brake. The rider is actively engaged in the process, and we do not want the horse to learn the pattern of ignoring a stop cue. The horse is immediately praised for stopping, no matter when it occurred.

I have observed many other programs and practitioners treat the horse as a tool and use them only in that capacity. We feel they are an intricate part of the therapeutic team. They have a special sense for what the client needs and are sensitive to the slightest balance issues long before any human team member. Our volunteers are taught to notice when the horse shows signs of discomfort — stopping after a few steps, tension in the nostrils or ears, widened eyes, or fast breathing. These are signs that they are communicating their own or the client's distress. We are dedicated to respecting what they are feeling and responding accordingly.

We stay stopped for at least five seconds so that halts do not become pauses. Horses and humans fall into patterns easily, and we need stop to mean stop. After several successful halts, our goal is to turn using focus, intention, and turning the torso — pointing the belly button exactly where we want the horse to go. We teach this through an exercise we call the "airplane exercise." The rider holds their arms out at shoulder height and turns like a robot, moving the whole torso at once. The hard part is keeping the nose, chin, and belly button aligned. The head tends to turn too far even when the eyes stay on the destination. It takes practice. If this does not work, I ask them to hold a riding stick at their belly button and turn their torso so the stick points in the direction they want to go.

We start with a walk and then find a nearby object to redirect to. We suggest a gentle turn to start. We halt at the object and find a new one to travel to. When they accomplish this, we move to weaving through three cones, then on to the slowest barrel race in the world. Eventually, we add cones to the tops of the barrels with rings on the cones. This exercise pulls together all the skills — focus, intention, turning, stopping, leaning forward to pull the ring off the cone, crossing the midline, and finishing the turn to focus on the next barrel. We make sure they understand how amazing it is that they can do this. Think of all that needed to be managed and regulated during that little piece of work. Some clients get it in a couple of weeks, and some take months. The key to success is meeting them where they are in the moment and building on their skills when they are ready.

At the end of every riding session, we do exercises. I have no particular reason for doing them at the end instead of the beginning. I like the peace of it — the tying together of what they learned — and perhaps it adds to the muscle building by doing one more thing. We often ask verbal clients what they learned during their time with the horse. And it is completely fine if they do not have an answer. I know that once I ask the question, they may only be able to answer in their heads and hearts.

When I look at the physical, emotional, and mental control needed for riding, I am amazed by what my clients can accomplish.

A neurotypical person is challenged to keep it all straight. Yet with time — and the love my special-needs children have for the horses — they too can develop body, emotional, and mental control.

The Exercises

All exercises are done with a person holding the lead rope of the horse. With clients with muscle tone and or balance issues, a second person stands next to them supporting them as needed.

Toe Twirls

This exercise has the child remove their feet from the stirrups and "draw" circles with each foot — or squares or triangles. This stretches and relaxes the ankles after having the feet in the stirrups. For some children, the very act of finding their feet and moving them is difficult. Some start with one foot, then move to the other. Then I have them twirl in the opposite direction. Most can twirl one direction more easily than the other. I remind them they can do this anytime their ankles get tired while riding.

Clicking Heels Over the Horse's Neck

This exercise builds upper-thigh strength, core engagement, balance, and proprioception. With feet out of the stirrups, clients place their hands behind their back, one on each side, and grab the cantle of the saddle. Then they lift both legs at once and try to have their feet meet above the horse's mane. This is difficult, and any effort is acknowledged. Even getting their knees to rest on the knee rolls of the English saddle or the fork of the western saddle is a great start. We can build on any effort. I have them try three times.

Clicking Heels Over the Horse's Croup

We tell clients this is an important exercise because it is part of the emergency dismount they will learn. If they need to dismount quickly and both legs are not cleared of the cantle, a knee can get stuck and cause them to fall under the horse. The goal is to get both legs above the horse's rump at the same time so they can push away and land safely.

There is some work involved in lifting their own rump slightly to clear the cantle and extend the legs straight behind. Clients with low muscle tone struggle with this, and it takes them a long time to get the hang of it. It takes the time it takes. This is a difficult exercise and requires practice. I do not teach the emergency dismount until they have this one down fairly well.

Around the World

The rider brings the right leg over the horse's neck and sits sideways on the left side. Then they swing the left leg over the horse's rump and sit backwards. Younger children love it when I tell them they cannot ride a horse like that. I often hear, "But you told me to!" I adore my literal thinkers.

Next, they swing the right leg over to sit on the right side, then swing the left leg over to return to the correct riding position. To complete the exercise, I tell them they are all wound up and I cannot send them home that way — so they must do it again in the opposite direction to unwind.

Froggy Sit

Riders use their core and balance to ride well. This exercise strengthens both. Riders lean back a couple of inches past center and lift their legs up and away from the saddle with knees bent. Hands stay up and away from holding the saddle or their legs. They breathe deeply and exhale slowly while holding the position as long as they can. Clients with muscle weakness may get a cramp in the outer thigh if they hold too long. I ask them to be aware of this and put their legs down if they feel a cramp coming on.

Standing in the Stirrups

Many clients tend to point their toes down and lose their balance while riding. This exercise helps them feel what happens when toes drop — the body automatically tips forward.

We help position the leg directly under the shoulder so a line drawn down from the shoulder goes through the hip and down the back of the lower leg. I ask them to imagine placing their whole foot on the ground rather than saying "toes up" or "heels down." Then they stand up, keeping knees and ankles soft. They do not need to stand fully upright, but their bottoms should be above the saddle. Once they can do this while standing still, we lead the horse at a walk. Eventually, they can do this at the walk and trot.

Reaching for the Poll

The poll is between the horse's ears. The client reaches forward with one hand and then the other as far as they can without leaning on the crest of the neck. Once they can do one hand at a time, we have them reach with both hands. Occasionally a client melts forward and rests on the horse's neck. I am fine with that — it relaxes their back and brings them into the horse's warmth and lovely smell. I do watch to ensure they do not get too far forward in case the horse lowers its head. No forward rolls off the horse at this stage — or ever.

Reaching for the Dock

The dock is the tailbone. The client reaches the left hand out, twists around, and leans back until their fingers touch the top of the tail. Then they sit up and repeat with the right hand. Once they do this easily, I may ask them to try touching the dock with both hands at the same time.

Toe Touches

I only start this exercise when I am sure they are strong enough to get back up from a bent-over position. I may ask them to touch their knees or shins before trying to touch their toes. We use the left hand to touch the right toe, then the right hand to touch the left toe. I have them do this three times on each side, alternating each time.

THE OUTCOME

As clients grow in skill and confidence, something remarkable begins to happen: the work shifts from "learning to ride" to "learning to be." The horse becomes a mirror, reflecting back the client's courage, their softness, their frustration, and their triumphs. In that reflection, clients begin to recognize parts of themselves they never knew were there — strength they didn't believe they had, calm they didn't think they could access, and a sense of belonging that often feels brand new. These moments, small and steady, are where transformation takes root. They are the quiet victories that build a bridge between the arena and the rest of their lives, reminding them that the partnership they create with the horse is also a partnership they can create with themselves.

Partnership with a horse is never just about riding. It is the weaving together of energy, intention, trust, and emotional presence — moment by moment, breath by breath. Every exercise, every pause at the mounting block, every quiet exhale is part of a larger conversation between two beings learning to meet each other with honesty and curiosity.

For many of my clients, this is the first place where their bodies, emotions, and thoughts begin to work together rather than against them. They discover that they can influence a thousand-pound animal with nothing more than focus and a steady breath. They learn that frustration can soften into problem-solving, that fear can settle into curiosity, and that connection — real connection — comes from showing up as they are.

The horse responds not to perfection, but to authenticity. And in that response, clients begin to recognize their own strength, their own capacity to regulate, to choose, to lead, and to trust. The skills they practice in the arena — awareness, empathy, intention, self-compassion — become the very skills that help them navigate the world beyond it.

The heart of Energy Connected Therapeutic Horsemanship is the partnership that grows both horse and human, creating new pathways of confidence, resilience, and joy. When a client dismounts at the end of a session — tired, proud, and glowing — they carry more than new skills. They carry the lived experience of being capable, connected, and whole.

And that is where the real transformation begins.

CHAPTER NINE

Q&A WITH MARCY – THE HUMAN STORY BEHIND THE WORK

"Everybody has a heart that can be touched by something."

~ Naoki Higashida, *The Reason I Jump*

There comes a point in this work when people begin to wonder not just *what* we do at That Zen Farm, but *why* it works the way it does. The horses, the breathwork, the sensory awareness, the quiet moments of connection — none of it is accidental. Every choice, every pause, every invitation to slow down or lean in is rooted in years of learning from the horses and from the remarkable humans who come here.

Before you meet the families whose stories fill the next chapter, I wanted to pause and answer a few of the questions I'm asked most often. These questions open a window into the heart of this work — the philosophy behind it, the challenges that shape it, and the deep respect I hold for every client who steps into the arena.

Think of this Q&A as a conversation on the rail: the horses breathing nearby, the dust settling, and the truth of the work rising to the surface. It's a moment to reflect before we step into the stories that show the work in motion.

Have you had to walk away from any client? What was that like?

I do not like to give up on anyone. If I have a prideful part of me, it would be my ability to get through to the most difficult clients. It does not always work. Usually — and I can only remember three or four — the client is someone who does not want to learn; they only want the sensory input of going faster on the horse and nothing more.

From my perspective, what we do here is build relationships — with the horse, with my volunteers, and with me. We help clients connect with more than their family, more than their therapists, and try something new and succeed. If the client shows no interest in the horse itself, we are not a good fit. I talk with the parent and may try one more time to see if we can spark interest. If not, we mutually agree that this is not a good fit.

I recently had a new client who was everywhere — climbing the fence rails, running after the cats, eating sand. The pony was in a smaller enclosure eating hay. The boy ran in, slid to a halt, and stood for a nanosecond by the pony's side. In that nanosecond, I knew we had a chance to make this work.

I invited them to come back and try again. I made some changes to accommodate him, to meet him where he is in this moment of his journey. I have the horse brushed and saddled when he arrives. We put the bridle on together and walk the horse around the arena together. Then we ride. When he reaches his filled-up point, we take the tack off together, and he brushes the pony to the best of his ability and feeds the cookies.

Eventually, as we progress, I will add more at the beginning. At this point in time, he cannot handle that much preparation — it is simply not in him.

What is it like talking with the parents of these children?

My goal is to empower them and support them on their journey of raising these beautiful, special children. While I know the horse best, they know the child best and can give me insights into what works and what does not. They, like most parents, are doing the best they can. The difference is that they are doing it twenty-four hours a day, seven days a week.

Some have trouble finding time for themselves because there are only a limited number of helpers who can take over for them, even for a short while. My heart goes out to them. They will be on this journey for a long time. Some of these kids will be in the home for most of their lives. Some will go on to college and a life on their own. Whatever their journey looks like, you can be sure these moms and dads will still be involved as much as they are allowed to be.

I have started doing mom support groups for when these overextended mothers get a chance to find some time to recuperate. We work on who they are so they can find themselves again — and find the strength to continue supporting their children on their journey.

Are the changes in the children long-lasting, or do they regress when they are no longer doing equine therapy?

I find that the changes in most cases last a long time. Sometimes, in the beginning, the child can stay regulated for a whole week. The down side is if they don't come a week they can regress in their behaviors. The parents can be sad about that. I don't give the parents a timeline or set expectations as to how long to bring their children to the farm. I leave that up to them. I have had children come for a summer and then never again, and I have had children spend years with the horses.

How long does a client typically stay in the program?

The decision to stay or go is up to the parents. Most of my equine therapy students are on a state- or county-sponsored (waiver) financial support program and they "graduate" either when they are eighteen years old or when they are vastly improved and it is determined they no longer require services. I have a couple who come even though they are no longer sponsored because they love it so much.

* * *

As much as I can explain the work we do here, the truest understanding comes from the people who have lived it. Every family who walks into the arena brings their own history, their own hopes, their own challenges, and their own quiet courage. The horses meet them exactly where they are, and together they create moments of connection that no amount of explanation can fully capture. In the next chapter, you'll hear directly from the families who have trusted us with their stories. Their voices, their breakthroughs, their grief, their joy — these are the real heartbeats of That Zen Farm.

CHAPTER TEN

CLIENT STORIES – THE WORK IN ACTION

"Sometimes you have to fly on blind faith."

~ Lindsey McKenna

Every horse who steps into the arena brings their own wisdom, and every person who walks beside them brings their own story. The work we do at That Zen Farm is never just about horsemanship or technique — it is about connection, courage, and the quiet, steady unfolding of trust. After sharing my own reflections in the previous chapter, it feels right to step back now and let the families speak for themselves.

What follows are the voices of parents, caregivers, and riders who have allowed me the privilege of walking part of their journey with them. Their stories are tender, honest, and full of the small miracles that happen when a human and a horse meet each other exactly where they are. Some of these stories are about transformation, some about healing, some about joy, and all of them are about relationship.

These families have given permission for their experiences to be shared, and I hold that trust with deep gratitude. Their words illuminate the heart of this work far better than any explanation I could offer. As you read, I invite you to slow down, breathe, and let their stories settle into you the way the horses settle into us — gently, steadily, and with great presence.

COLIN'S STORY

Colin came to That Zen Farm in April of 2019. It was the only place around with a horse large enough for this amazing and growing young man. He has a gentle soul and a true love for animals. He absorbs facts like a sponge, and when he met Snowman, he wanted to know everything.

Snowman was a rescue from Spirit Horse Equine Rescue and Education Center. He was surrendered when his rider went off to college and could no longer care for him. He was a beautiful gray Percheron–Quarter Horse of middle age and as sweet as the day was long.

The day before the surrender clinic, he had jumped a fence and injured his abdomen. The veterinarians were unsure how extensive the damage was. The outside injuries were a long, deep edema running along his belly. They were not sure he would survive. He was scheduled to be euthanized that day. DeeDee, the heart and soul of the rescue, loaded him up and brought him back to the home farm to give him a chance to live. And live he did. I met him when we began working together to prepare for a demonstration at a fundraising event. I fell under his spell and soon asked to adopt him.

Snowman and Colin began to get to know each other. Colin was always worried that his weight was too much for the horse. It was borderline with Snowman, so we worked on the ground much of our time together. Colin learned to groom, tack up, and read horse body language and emotions. He learned to wait for the shy horse to want to do things with him and to enjoy being with him. He did ride Snowman a few times and had a huge grin on his face each time.

We retired Snowman in 2020. Sadly, one day in 2021, he colicked and died very suddenly. He was about twenty-five years old, which is old for a draft horse. We all grieved for a long time. Some days I still see him, in my mind's eye, watching us in his calming way.

In November of 2020, we brought Maya Moose home from Nebraska. She is a Clydesdale — huge and beautiful. When the government allowed us to return to work in 2021, we started working with Maya and Colin. He had found a new friend. Maya, he discovered, is a much larger horse and a completely different personality than Snowman. She had trouble being in the indoor arena, and we worked a long time to reassure her that she was safe. Even with her best friend Dazzle beside her, she was skeptical of the place. Colin worked with her with steady confidence and peace. He helped her overcome her dislike of being saddled and taught her to stand at the mounting block with patience. He even chose to ride her on occasion. He still says he is too big. His goal, he says, is to learn about the horse — riding is not that important to him.

He once told me that Maya was like the girl who sits at the front of the classroom with her hand up for every answer, and Snowman was like the boy hiding at the back with his hoodie covering his face. He was right — an amazing observation on his part. Even more amazing was his realization that what worked with Snowman did not necessarily work with Maya.

Colin recently aged out of the program that was paying for his time here. He now comes occasionally to work with Maya. I interviewed him to discover what he felt he had gained in his five years here.

Colin said he had only one encounter with a pony before he came. He said horses helped him learn patience and read body language. "Now it's the first thing I look at with animals. Before, I didn't pay any attention to it." He said he learned how to walk, to look forward and walk tall, and to focus on where he was going.

"My knowledge of horses is great now. It's too bad I can't flex my knowledge at my job at the farm sanctuary where I work — they only have one tiny dwarf mini."

"Being here has given me confidence to do my job. Learning body language has helped me understand animals who have been abused. I learned that animals are individuals, and some didn't get their own preferences."

When asked what he would still like to learn, he replied that he is always willing to learn almost anything. "I'm not yet a master of understanding horses."

He said he leaves here every time in a better mood and more relaxed than when he arrived. "I just like them and being with them."

Colin's parents added the following:

> We knew immediately that the horsemanship skills you taught — versus the traditional style — were absolutely the right method for Colin. Being on the autism spectrum, reading social cues and body language was not an innate or natural skill he possessed. Working with Snowman — assessing his readiness to engage in lessons, be brushed, be saddled, show regulation through licking, chewing, sighing, and other signs — was the very best way for him to practice these skills. Because of his connection with animals, this was the perfect way to work on goals we had struggled to meet in therapy elsewhere.
>
> Colin is a boy who never wears anything on his feet other than Crocs, with no socks. When working with Snowman, we were able to slowly transition him to stable and arena shoe choices — socks and shoes, and eventually boots. Although he is still unable to tie his shoes, he was excited enough to work with the horses that he no longer fought wearing the appropriate footwear.

Car rides were also incredibly difficult, especially long rides with winding roads. He suffers from vestibular issues, dizziness, and motion sickness. Colin was willing to make the forty-minute drive one way to see his horse. Although it did not cure his sickness, it gave him a favored activity that allowed him to build adaptive skills. He found that if he fell asleep in the car, he was no longer sick and could tolerate longer rides. This opened many more options for activities. We have now driven to Chicago and other places we never dreamed possible — two or three hours away — to see museums and other activities he once missed due to car sickness.

Losing Snowman was also a beautiful experience that allowed Colin to work through incredibly difficult emotions. I remember you telling him at his last visit with Snowman that he 'didn't need to say it out loud — he could say it in his head and Snowman would hear it,' as horses are telepathic. This helped him understand that you can think things without always verbalizing them. It helped him later verbalize those words. This has come up many times at his internship at the animal sanctuary, where multiple animals have passed.

He has been able to spend time with animals at the end of their lives and provide comfort, love, and compassion in their final days. We believe this helped him work through many of the sad, scared, and devastating emotions he experienced during his father's nearly life-ending illnesses from 2019 to 2020. Not everyone is meant to sit with others during devastatingly sad times, but this helped Colin offer that gift to both humans and animals.

Lastly, one of the most important pieces is the absolute joy the horses brought to Colin. He always knew he could come to the farm and be greeted by you, Marcy — a nonjudgmental, compassionate, and kind listener and teacher. He felt safe enough to talk about all sorts of issues with you, and you always listened to his information dumps, offered your opinion, and guided him back to caring for and interacting with the horse. We knew that every single Monday (and Tuesday too) would be filled with nonstop stories about Snowman and Maya Moose. He felt Snowman was one of his very best friends in the world. They had an incredible connection that brought Colin so much joy.

His experience with Snowman solidified his gift for working with animals and has now led to an internship at an animal sanctuary, which will eventually lead to a paid position. Starting with the horses laid all the groundwork — joy, engagement, reading body language, working through challenges that once seemed unachievable, more joy, laughter, lots of horse dirt, and the ability to understand the concept of consent. He learned that each living being has the ability to like or not like something — and if you look closely and try to understand their way of explaining it, they will let you know.

KAPIL'S STORY

Kapil first came here in August of 2019 and was frightened of everything farm — chickens, cats, dogs, and horses. The cats were the worst. It has been nearly five years, and he is just now starting to pet them if I am holding them.

We started him with Cotton Candi, the gentlest pony in the world. Kapil, as intelligent as he is, lived in adrenaline mode when he first started here. It was so hard for him to relax and learn when his internal alarm system was constantly going off. Who could learn in that state? In my opinion, no one. We started slowly — petting, then brushing, then saddling and riding. Each step was taken with patience and care to maintain his self-respect and learning path.

We use an easy obstacle course to teach our riders. This teaches planning, focus, intention, self-regulation, and the feeling of success. We add to the obstacles or make them harder as each challenge is met and conquered. He is now riding independently and has conquered our inside and outside obstacle courses. I cannot wait to see how he does with our new challenges.

When Candi passed, he graduated to a bigger pony. Naughty John is aptly named. He tests just enough to keep his riders on task but is super friendly and a charmer. Kapil had to increase his awareness, pay more attention, strengthen his leadership skills, and have patience with himself and the horse. Kapil now rides with either an English saddle or a bareback pad.

As he grew in height and through practice, practice, practice, he now does nearly all the tasks to prepare, ride, and send the horse back home. His confidence and ability to stay in the moment and remain aware have grown over time. We are working on picking up the horse's hoof and cleaning it out. This is particularly hard for him, as he still fears being stepped on. It has never happened, and yet the fear remains. He must trust the teachers, the horse, and himself — and that is hard to do. Each time, we add a little more to what he can do. The beautiful thing about Kapil is that he always comes back and goes a bit further. It is one of the things I admire most about this young man.

Recently, during one of our sessions, a sudden screeching, ear-splitting noise came from across the road at our neighbor's house — it turned out to be a saw on aluminum siding. Naughty John stopped suddenly and froze. I asked Kapil what he "read" in his horse. He replied that John was scared, and so was he. I asked what he thought he should do next. He said he thought he should get down because it was not safe. I agreed, and he got down and untacked the horse.

So many things were revealed in that less-than-a-minute conversation. Kapil read the horse's emotions and reaction to the unusual sound. He understood the danger of being on a horse running on adrenaline. He recognized his own fear and that it could add to the horse's fear. He made the decision to get down through logic — not fear. To me, all of that is huge. He showed me that he will grow into an amazing horseman with empathy and grace.

I recently asked Kapil what he had learned about himself since he started here. He said, "I can ride independently, and I learned flexibility. The horses gave me a lot of patience and more courage. I can communicate with horses, and that helped me communicate with people. I learned to read body language. I learned a lot of lessons — like to control my energy and my emotions. If I get scared, the horse can get scared. They understand my emotions."

Kapil's parents, Sid and Deepti, added the following:

> Our son, Kapil, was a timid and reclusive ten-year-old when he started hippotherapy (coaching) with Marcy. His fear of animals was such that he refused to play in the park to avoid encounters with dogs. We had two Ragdoll cats at home, and he was a little more comfortable with them. However, his heightened sensory defensiveness and overwhelming fear of unpredictability kept him from truly relaxing in their presence. For these reasons, we were not surprised to see his trepidation around the horses on his first day at Marcy's riding therapy school.
>
> Despite his fears, the first session was astonishing. Marcy built a bond of trust with Kapil right away and, through patience and gentle encouragement, even got him to

touch the pony. She asked him if he would come back for more before we left, and it was heartwarming to see him nod with enthusiasm. Once the sessions began, they quickly became the highlight of his week. Kapil had no friends in or outside school and struggled with socializing with same-age peers. Therefore, the growing bond with Marcy and Cotton Candi (his first pony) became his only connections outside our family.

Once he began to sit on the horse, it also became a source of self-esteem for him. He would proudly tell people about horseback riding when asked about his hobbies. We, as parents, were immensely grateful for the confidence and positive spirit that Marcy was able to build in Kapil because of how little he received in terms of validation from the world outside our home. Kapil could always count a strong work ethic and a love for learning among his strengths, but working with horses brought out his latent qualities — the courage to try something new and the beginnings of empathy. Since perspective-taking and understanding nonverbal cues were areas where he struggled most, we were particularly pleased to see him emotionally bond with his pony and try to sense what she was feeling.

The last five years with Marcy and her horses have been a long and beautiful journey with many blessings and a few inevitable setbacks for Kapil. Among the latter was the passing of Candi, Kapil's first pony and the gentlest of creatures. He was heartbroken by the loss but was able to carry forward with his learning through a lot of support from Marcy. He is now equally fond of Naughty John and looks forward to seeing him all week.

He has also developed the flexibility to work with other horses if his own is not available — a remarkable improvement for a boy deeply attached to his routines.

Looking back, it is almost incredible to us how far Kapil has come since that first day in the summer of 2019. He has blossomed as a person and a rider by building empathy, self-confidence, and trust under Marcy's experienced tutelage. We are so proud of him and look forward to seeing him continue to grow as a human being. We are deeply grateful to Marcy for all the tangible and intangible ways she has supported our son and helped him expand his vision of himself and what is possible. It is her faith in him as a student and his trust in her as a teacher that has made all the difference.

CALEB'S STORY

By Rachel Seay

I was looking for a place for my son, Caleb, to ride and be around horses and other animals. Caleb has ASD and ADHD, as well as a history of mental-health challenges. Our family case worker connected us to Marcy and her farm. Caleb was about fourteen years old at the time. He has loved animals ever since he was small, and animals have always loved him back. I had horses as a child, so I knew there was something special about these creatures, but I never fully understood it the way I do after being at Marcy's farm.

Caleb rode Billy Bob for the first few sessions and then was introduced to Maya, the Clydesdale. I remember Marcy telling Caleb that he was going to help work with Maya.

Caleb learned how to read Maya and how to show her that she could trust him. They now have a very special bond. Caleb also enjoys the cats and the chickens.

Caleb had always struggled to understand the social aspects of people. He suffered traumas at a school that did not understand his needs. I knew he felt depleted and had lost confidence in himself. He would get frustrated and angry at school and at other activities I had tried to enroll him in. I could tell he so badly wanted to participate, but he needed to be in a place where he was understood — who he is and where he is in this moment. And it was incredibly hard to find that fit for him.

Watching him work with Maya and being so eager to learn everything Marcy was teaching him, I started to see the Caleb I knew reemerge. He became calm around the horses, and his confidence began to grow. Each week Marcy asks if he wants to use a saddle or a bareback pad. Caleb always chooses the bareback pad. So here is Caleb, riding a Clydesdale bareback with just reins attached to a rope halter. But wow — I wish I had that kind of courage.

At the end of eighth grade, Caleb came home from school one day and said he had signed up for the football team for his freshman year of high school. I thought, *What?* Every sport he had ever tried ended in tears and frustration. *How is he going to do this?* Never in a million years would I have thought he would come home and say he was going out for football. He attended the camps and practices that summer — and he loved it.

It was one of my proudest moments, sitting in the stands and seeing him on the football field. It was like all the dots connected for him. I found out he has been quite sociable at school and has lots of friends. Maya was able to gift Caleb with so much. Marcy has the knowledge of horses and how they relate and speak to humans, the understanding of special-needs children, and the beautiful gift of meeting both people and horses where they are and building up from there.

Caleb not only found his confidence, but I noticed he was starting to recognize body language better and show compassion outwardly. He has turned into a very chill, easygoing kind of guy. He knows what he needs to do for himself. I am truly a believer in Marcy's miracle program.

EMBER'S STORY

By Jason Collet

I am writing this for two reasons. One is to serve as an accounting and reflection of my daughter's experience with equestrian therapy. The other is to hopefully offer something of value to another parent who is considering such therapy for their child.

To begin with, my daughter's name is Ember. She is bright, beautiful, willful, resourceful, sweet, kind, and very, very clever. She is also autistic, which presents specific challenges and difficulties. A person might say that my daughter is severely autistic, although I must admit that I am not much for broad-stroke labels such as "high functioning," "low functioning," or "Asperger's." Ember's primary challenge is that she is nonverbal, which I have found is the key factor in how the world perceives a person's autistic traits. My daughter lacks her voice, but she has no shortage of critical thinking, empathy, or intuition. This combination generates anxiety, as she finds herself unable to express the things she is clearly seeing and feeling.

I have watched with wistful pride as my daughter has made tremendous strides in overcoming the trials and tribulations that autism presents for her. It is a key life goal of mine to provide her with as many tools as possible to create her own happiness — her own solace in life. It was in this step of her journey that we began, this last year, with her equestrian therapy.

Like any parent of an autistic child, my wife and I have read innumerable articles in our search to improve her life. There are anecdotes for just about everything — a special diet that was "a game changer," some oil additive or cleansing treatment that restored speech within hours, and of course various therapies and interventions. Among these were always stories of autistic children who found something grounding and powerful while riding horses. Given that both my wife and I had some background with horses, we understood the potential of such wonderfully empathic beings bonding with our daughter and providing her outlets for creativity, agency, and most of all, contentedness. We moved our family to Wisconsin in large part to expose Ember to this experience.

There is a common saying: "If you know a child with autism, you know exactly one child with autism." While both my wife and I were hopeful that equestrian therapy would be a good experience for Ember, we were guardedly optimistic. We have learned over the years that some things simply do not click for Ember — sometimes even things that seem to work for nearly every other autistic child. Hope is a powerful, double-edged sword, with deep disappointment on the other side if you let expectations run too wild.

We researched extensively, knowing how important it is to start on the right note and not let an early bad experience poison future possibilities. After speaking with many peers and social workers, we settled on a place near Oregon (which I was told emphatically is pronounced "OreeGONE") called That Zen Farm. We made our appointments and tried to keep our excitement in check.

Our first day at the farm was surreal. Snow was everywhere, it was bitterly cold, and Ember did not seem like she wanted to get out of the car. What's more, she was incredibly spooked by the cats roaming about. I was steeling myself for the very real possibility that this just was not going to work out. But then we met Marcy — and Billy, the horse.

Something that surprised me in the arena was the complete and utter sense of calm. It was a different experience for Ember, yes, but there was no anxiety to be felt. This was likely in no small part because I felt no anxiety, and my daughter — who is powerfully empathic — did not pick it up from me. Most new experiences fill us both with anxiety, as there are other people around and many things to consider. Will Ember have a meltdown? Will we be able to resolve any issues on the spot, or will we have to leave? Will the people nearby understand? None of these questions mattered in the arena. If Ember had an issue, it would simply be something that happened. That level of acceptance and simplicity provided the first true glimpse of what this therapy offered.

Ember's instructor, Marcy, embodied this feeling in the flesh. I am used to many people establishing a strong connection with Ember — she is sweet and quite a charmer. What struck me about Marcy, however, is that while she is fond of Ember, she has a deeper love for the work she does. From the first meeting to every session thereafter, Marcy's tone, patience, and rooted understanding of what this therapy is resonated with Ember completely. There would be days that were better than others — this was understood. There was also an understanding that the horse's empathic connection with the kids was more than a benefit; it was a compass.

Whereas I had focused on Ember learning how to ride and care for a horse, the therapy was much more about assisting her in simply being in the moment. This is something I fear I forget with my daughter in my drive to help her improve and achieve her goals — sometimes a kid just needs to have fun and be a kid. As such, I have watched Ember improve her balance, dexterity, posture, and receptive language for instructions. But I have also watched her smile softly at the simple bounce of trotting, take in a deep breath of the heady scent of hay and horses, and grin as she spelled her name with the hairbrush on the horse's flank instead of actually removing hair.

There have been lessons for me as well. A big one has been learning to let things develop and progress without interceding in everything. From this, Ember has shown she is quite capable of building rapport and taking direction from others. Most days I stay on the sidelines and watch Marcy and Ember do their thing. I have also been reminded that progress is a marathon, not a sprint. Over this last year, Ember has built on her fundamentals for horseback riding across areas I did not initially expect — her balance, flexibility, and endurance have all gradually improved and strengthened.

We have switched between two horses this past year, Billy and John. They have their own distinct personalities and quirks. Marcy knows them as well as she might her own children. There have also been a number of volunteer assistants, each contributing their own unique strengths.

Ember's journey into equestrian therapy has just begun. We are just past a year of going to That Zen Farm, and I expect this will be something she enjoys for many years. I do not know if this will become something Ember truly resonates with and wants to take to the next level. She is certainly athletic enough should she choose to pursue horseback riding more seriously. In our quest to find things that invigorate and capture her curiosity, this would be a wonderful catalyst.

Regardless, this time and energy investment has been exceptional for Ember, and I am grateful for the opportunity to share a recounting of it with anyone.

LUCIA'S STORY

By Tessa Richardson, LCSW

Our seven-year-old daughter came to That Zen Farm with an autism diagnosis and a lot of worries for such a small person. When she is working with Marcy, I can almost see her nervous system downshifting as she co-regulates with the horses and with Marcy's steady, calm, and kind presence. The horses seem to have an innate ability to connect with our child, offering a supportive environment that fosters growth and confidence.

Our daughter has always struggled with self-esteem and emotional regulation. With patience and expertise, Marcy has guided her through various activities, helping her build trust, develop communication skills, and gain a newfound sense of self-confidence. It has been a gift to witness the positive changes and growth in her since starting these sessions.

The bond she is forming with the horses is gentle and sweet. It is evident that the horses are more than just animals; they are genuine partners in her journey. Each session is filled with courage, learning, and a sense of accomplishment she has not experienced before.

Overall, That Zen Farm has been such a gift for our family. The positive impact on our daughter's confidence and emotional regulation is clear, and I wholeheartedly recommend this place to any family seeking a compassionate and effective approach to therapy.

MY DAUGHTERS' STORY

By Emily Boone

Some years ago, a sleep-deprived, overwhelmed mom of five-year-old twins and a toddler — whose father was navigating acute leukemia in another state — was trying to get her dysregulated, not-yet-known-as-autistic five-year-old child into a car seat. We were leaving a session with Marcy, and transitions away from comfort were especially rough for a neurodivergent child. All of a sudden, I heard a voice calling from the house about one hundred feet away: "Ma'am, remember to breathe!" Such a simple instruction, but in that moment it was a powerful intervention. As a parent, it is easy to forget our own basic needs while trying to support a child. Marcy's playful reminder has been tattooed on my consciousness — eight years later, I still think of her holding me in wisdom and care.

In this moment, as I sit by the side of the arena, I have the immense privilege of witnessing Marcy teach my now nine- and thirteen-year-olds how to use their breath to communicate with the horse. My children use the power of their exhales, tapping into their parasympathetic nervous systems, to connect in relationship with nine-hundred-pound beings.

These outbreaths are no small miracles. My children have survived multiple challenges — from being born two months early, to being bullied and assaulted at school, to more recently navigating multiple surgeries for an abdominal tumor. Enough to make a mom's breath stop.

But here we are on a gorgeous late-summer afternoon, co-regulating and finding joy in relationships with horses and humans. I know it is technically my children who are receiving lessons from Marcy and her skillful assistants, Laura and Sybil, but I can feel in my own nervous system how impactful being in their presence is on me too.

On a recent afternoon en route to Marcy's, I found myself feeling time-pressured and disturbed by the plethora of election signs supporting candidates who, let's just say, see the world very differently than I do.

Within five minutes of being greeted by a crew of scrappy and charismatic barn cats, warm humans, and brilliant horses, my nervous system was no longer in a sympathetic state.

I watch my daughter — in a tearful puddle of pre-start-of-school anxiety — as her body relaxes into the saddle. She is riding Nein, a horse who knows his own trauma. Together they co-regulate in spite of the flies, the impending start of school, the past surgical trauma, and the election signs representing another way of seeing things.

Marcy told me that horses are biologically set up to eat about twenty hours per day, and that they need to be stress-free to do so. They also want the whole herd to be stress-free. Safety is required for digestion. These creatures have evolved to support one another in community. The well-being of one is the well-being of all. Can you imagine if we humans saw one another this way?

Marcy teaches my children about the horses' unique sensory preferences and needs — about what scares them and what delights them. In turn, my children are invited to feel a sense of belonging in their own bodily needs and experiences. Meeting the horses with compassion helps us all relate to ourselves with more compassion, warmth, and curiosity when we are having a hard time.

At one point in the lesson, Marcy invites my daughter to help support a sweet but slightly reluctant horse to continue moving: "Set your intention to move like a bubble in front of you." With evocative and playful imagery, Marcy engages the imagination — a part of our nervous system essential not just for safety but also for healing and connection.

On the drive home, I feel myself contract slightly as I pass election signs. My nine-year-old in the back seat easily picks up on this and tells me, "Mama, breathe in what you believe and exhale those Trump signs."

POSY'S STORY

By Scott Oakwell

Posy is a neurotypical young girl who is bright, has a lovely personality, and holds a great love for the animals at That Zen Farm. Posy started at That Zen Farm with challenges around self-worth, sense of self, self-confidence, and decision-making. We noticed a definite gain in all those areas, as well as her finding her voice. She can now express how she feels in a situation — something that was hard for her to put into words before.

In our day-to-day life, whether it is school, family issues, friend problems, or self-confidence struggles, I have seen Posy use skills learned at That Zen Farm to face her problems head-on.

When Posy's siblings have been disappointed by something, I have heard her say, "One time when I was riding at the farm, I messed up when I was trying to go around a barrel, but I kept trying and Marcy helped me and I got it right and I felt so happy! It's okay to be disappointed, but keep trying." Posy's ability to connect moments when she has been scared (like getting down from the saddle) or felt she failed (like learning to post the trot), yet kept trying and improved, is amazing. I believe this growth is a direct result of her time at That Zen Farm and her work with Marcy.

Secondly — and perhaps the biggest change — is Posy's ability to make decisions. Anytime she has a decision to make at home, I will say, "Pretend you are on a horse, and you need to make the decision so your horse knows where to go." That turns a twenty-minute period of uncertainty into a five-minute process. It is good to make considerations when making decisions, but in the past Posy struggled with self-doubt and confidence. Thinking of her choices as if she were guiding a horse seems to help her tremendously.

We appreciate the time Marcy spends with us and with Posy. We thank her for creating a space where Posy has gained so much.

ANONYMOUS CLIENT EXPERIENCE

By Jen Bluske, OT and owner of Children's Therapy Network, Madison, Wisconsin

The little boy shows up and, without a moment of hesitation, enters the arena with a big smile on his face. His comfort is clear. His excitement is clear. Marcy is able to keep the momentum of him entering the arena and gently move him into the routine. The little guy really likes the cat and is a bit distracted by it. However, Marcy is able to honor the little boy and his experience while using her presence, intonation, and body positioning to keep him directed toward the task at hand — brushing the horse.

Right away, I can see the richness of the sensory experience for this little boy and how Marcy helps him make sense of the varied sensory input inherent in all interactions with the horse. He starts by grooming — brushing Whinnie round and round. When the round-and-round motion is tricky,

Marcy effortlessly steps in and provides a motor prompt to help his body learn the movement. He is then able to complete it independently. One of the most exciting parts of grooming is the banging of the brush on the wall. There is some limit-setting and negotiation, which Marcy handles while maintaining connection and the joy inherent in the activity. The little boy runs his fingers through the horse's mane but quickly returns to the task at hand. Marcy uses language to label the experiences, but the power is in her choice of *when* to use language. She often creates quiet moments of experience and connection, allowing the little boy to feel the fur, watch the swinging of the tail, and simply be in the moment.

They move on to preparing to ride. While I have never met this child, I imagine the idea of putting on a helmet is unusual, if not uncomfortable. However, because of Marcy's pacing, her clear cues about what is coming next, and her attunement to the subtle shifts in the little boy, the helmet goes on with no issue.

Tacking up a horse is inherently a motor-planning challenge. There are so many mini-steps that must be done in a specific order — and done correctly — to ensure the ride is safe and enjoyable. Again, Marcy paces the activity to meet the little boy's natural rhythm, allowing him to problem-solve the steps as independently as possible. At one point he puts the saddle pad on backward. Marcy engagingly cues, "Uh oh," and the little boy orients to the issue and fixes it. When necessary, she gives short, direct cues that match his language-processing skills.

They go for a walk next. It is clearly challenging for the little boy to orient his body in the preferred position relative to both Marcy and the horse. While he is supposed to be guiding Whinnie, in effect Marcy is supporting Whinnie to cue the little boy with increasing spatial awareness and appropriate walking speed. When the little boy becomes briefly distracted by the sand, Whinnie gently moves imperceptibly closer, redirecting him back to the task at hand.

Now the little boy is on the horse. Marcy continues to pace and co-regulate the experience, allowing for some choice in guiding the horse while subtly pushing for increased balance, improved guidance, and better motor-planning — full integration of the body.

Not mentioned explicitly is all the gross-motor and bodyawareness work Marcy is facilitating. What makes this special is that while balance, bilateral coordination, and trunk rotation can be cued in many ways, the feedback the horse provides helps the motor change truly "sit" in the body. After some more "horse gymnastics," Marcy looks at me and says he has reached his max. She is noticing the most subtle processing cues and movement shifts to determine when the lesson should end — ending on a positive.

This lesson is not Marcy's agenda. It is her holding the joy, curiosity, and exploration of the little boy she is working with, helping him ultimately learn that he is his own best advocate.

* * *

As you've just read, every story that unfolds at That Zen Farm is its own small universe — shaped by courage, curiosity, heartbreak, humor, and the quiet wisdom of the horses. These families have trusted me with their children, their hopes, their fears, their triumphs, and their voices, all of which form the heartbeat of this work. Their experiences are not just testimonials; they are living proof of what becomes possible when connection is honored, and every nervous system — human or horse — is met with respect. As we move into the final chapter, I invite you to carry these stories with you. They are the foundation of the legacy I hope to leave behind, and the clearest expression of why this work matters.

CONCLUSION

THE LEGACY I'D LIKE TO LEAVE BEHIND

"Horses lend us the wings we lack."

~ Pam Brown Marcy

Every story in the previous chapter carries a piece of my heart, because each one reflects what I have always hoped this place could be: a sanctuary where people and horses meet each other with honesty, curiosity, and compassion. As I look back on the years of teaching, learning, laughing, grieving, and growing alongside so many remarkable humans and horses, I find myself thinking more and more about what remains after the dust settles in the arena. What endures when the lessons are over, the children grow up, and the horses who shaped us move on to whatever comes next.

I would like to be remembered as kind, loving, and fully present in my work with all clients. Yet legacy is much more than being remembered. It is about what continues to ripple outward long after a moment has passed.

I hope to have like-minded people take over and continue to grow this work in the future. My plan is to invite Equine Gestalt coaches to work out of my arena and with my horses if they have none of their own. I would also like to train more teachers to work with special-needs families using my Energy Connected Therapeutic Horsemanship program.

More than anything, I hope to leave not only an enduring, peaceful place for people to find their true and unique selves but also a legacy of love, laughter, and confidence in the lives of those I touched. Legacy is the confidence a child carries into the world because a horse once trusted them. It is the breath a parent remembers to take because someone reminded them they deserved gentleness too. It is the quiet courage that grows when a person learns to listen to their own body the way they once listened to a horse's.

To all who have taken that journey here, I thank you for everything you have taught me about myself and the world around me.

May this place, and the beings who inhabit it, continue to offer the kind of quiet healing that lasts long after the gate closes behind you.

ABOUT THAT ZEN FARM AND THE AUTHOR

That Zen Farm, located in rural Brooklyn, Wisconsin, is the fulfillment of a lifelong dream: to bring the beauty and grace of horses into people's lives and to offer a peaceful, grounded place where children and adults can grow, heal, and discover new pathways forward. It is a sanctuary where the horse's innate wisdom meets the human need for connection, regulation, and authentic self-expression.

Its founder, Marcy Waelti, returned to school at age forty to study childcare and child development and went on to spend twenty-five years in the field of early childhood education, working with both typically and non-typically developing children. In 1998, she opened her horsemanship program to children with special needs, creating a space where learning, movement, and emotional safety could unfold at each child's pace.

In 2019, Marcy discovered the Touched By A Horse Equine Gestalt Coaching Method program and began her training in it. She completed the two-year certification program in 2021, expanding her work to include adults and older teens. In 2024, she earned an additional two-year certification in advanced Gestalt training, again through Touched By A Horse. With these combined modalities, her vision of supporting people across all ages and stages of development became fully realized.

Today, That Zen Farm stands as a place to find self-awareness, self-compassion, and the reminder that every person is already whole and capable. Through the partnership of horses, skilled coaching, and a deeply nurturing environment, clients are invited to reconnect with themselves in ways that are both gentle and transformative.

FINANCIAL SUPPORT

Check with the health and human services programs in your state or county for information on financial support for equine therapy.

CONTACT MARCY

Website: www.thatzenfarm.com
Email: marcy@thatzenfarm.com
Phone or WhatsApp: 608-575-2176
Facebook: That Zen Farm or Marcy Waelti
Instagram: That Zen Farm (thatzenfarm1) or Marcy Waelti (marcy.waelti)
Linked In: Marcy Waelti

RESOURCES

Touched by a Horse Equine Gestalt Coaching Certification Program. Accessed February 15, 2026. https://touchedbyahorse.com/

Gabriels, Robin L., Zhaoxing Pan, Briar Dechant, John A. Agnew, Natalie Brim, and Gary Mesibov. "Randomized Controlled Trial of Therapeutic Horseback Riding in Children and Adolescents With Autism Spectrum Disorder." *Journal of the American Academy of Child & Adolescent Psychiatry*, Vol. 54, no.7 (2015): 541-49, 2015.

Dreher, Diane E. "Why Do Horses Help Us Heal? The Promise of Equine Therapy." *Psychology Today*, January 6, 2018.

Rothe, E. Q., B. J. Vega, R. M. Torres, S. M. C. Soler, and R. M. M. Pazos. "From Kids and Horses: Equine-Facilitated Psychotherapy for Children." *International Journal of Clinical and Health Psychology*, Vol. 5 (2005): 373-83.

Sarris, Marina. "Something about a Horse: Finding Benefits for Autism in Therapeutic Riding." *SPARK for Autism*, September 26, 2022. https://sparkforautism.org/discover_article/something-about-a-horse-finding-benefits-for-autism-in-therapeutic-riding/.

Srinivasan, Sudha M., David T. Cavagnino, and Anjana N. Bhat. "Effects of Equine Therapy on Individuals with Autism Spectrum Disorder: A Systematic Review." *Review Journal of Autism and*

Developmental Disorders, Vol. 5, no. 2 (June 2018): 156-75. https://www.ncbi.nlm.nih.gov/pmc/articles/PMC6178825/.

Xiao, Ningkun, Khyber Shinwari, Sergey Kiselev, Xinlin Huang, Baoheng Li, and Jingjing Qi. "Effects of Equine-Assisted Activities and Therapies for Individuals with Autism Spectrum Disorder: Systematic Review and Meta-Analysis." *International Journal of Environmental Research and Public Health,* Vol. 20, no. 3 (February 1, 2023): article 2630. https://www.ncbi.nlm.nih.gov/pmc/articles/PMC9915993/.

Kershaw, Alicia. "Horseback Riding as Autism Therapy." *Autism Speaks*, accessed February 15, 2026. https://www.autismspeaks.org/expert-opinion/equine-therapy-autism/.

"Neurodiversity Quotes—Embracing the Beauty of Different Minds." *QuotePoem*. Accessed February 15, 2026. https://quotepoem.com/neurodiversity-quotes-embracing-the-beauty-of-different-minds/.

www.ingramcontent.com/pod-product-compliance
Lightning Source LLC
Chambersburg PA
CBHW071341230926
51846CB00002B/410
9781954102361